Success Secrets of Sherlock Holmes

SUCCESS SECRETS OF
Sherlock Holmes

Life Lessons
from the
Master Detective

David Acord

A PERIGEE BOOK

A PERIGEE BOOK
Published by the Penguin Group
Penguin Group (USA) Inc.
375 Hudson Street, New York, New York 10014, USA

Penguin Group (Canada), 90 Eglinton Avenue East, Suite 700, Toronto, Ontario M4P 2Y3, Canada (a division of Pearson Penguin Canada Inc.) • Penguin Books Ltd., 80 Strand, London WC2R 0RL, England • Penguin Group Ireland, 25 St. Stephen's Green, Dublin 2, Ireland (a division of Penguin Books Ltd.) • Penguin Group (Australia), 250 Camberwell Road, Camberwell, Victoria 3124, Australia (a division of Pearson Australia Group Pty. Ltd.) • Penguin Books India Pvt. Ltd., 11 Community Centre, Panchsheel Park, New Delhi—110 017, India • Penguin Group (NZ), 67 Apollo Drive, Rosedale, Auckland 0632, New Zealand (a division of Pearson New Zealand Ltd.) • Penguin Books (South Africa) (Pty.) Ltd., 24 Sturdee Avenue, Rosebank, Johannesburg 2196, South Africa

Penguin Books Ltd., Registered Offices: 80 Strand, London WC2R 0RL, England

Copyright © 2011 by David Acord
Text design by Kristin del Rosario

First edition: November 2011

Library of Congress Cataloging-in-Publication Data

Acord, David.
Success secrets of Sherlock Holmes : life lessons from the master detective / David Acord. — 1st ed.
    p. cm.
Includes bibliographical references and index.
ISBN 978-0-399-53698-4
   1. Doyle, Arthur Conan, Sir, 1859–1930—Characters—Sherlock Holmes.
2. Doyle, Arthur Conan, Sir, 1859–1930—Philosophy.   3. Holmes, Sherlock
(Fictitious character—Miscellanea.   4. Private investigators in literature.   I. Title.
   PR4624.A216   2011
   823'.8—dc22   2011008296

PRINTED IN THE UNITED STATES OF AMERICA
10 9 8 7 6 5 4 3 2 1

Contents

Contents

Contents

Acknowledgments

This project has been several years in the making, and it couldn't have happened without the help of two people in particular. I want to thank my agent, Sandy Choron, for believing in the idea from the very beginning. Her enthusiasm is infectious, and she worked tirelessly to find this book a home.

Second, I want to thank my editor, Meg Leder, for exhibiting patience above and beyond the call of duty. Authors can be notoriously flaky, and unfortunately I lived up (or down) to that reputation on more than one occasion, but for some reason Meg decided not to throw me off the nearest bridge. Her clear eye and keen sense of structure helped me create a much better book. If at any point in reading this book, you stop and say "Wow, I never thought of that!" chances are you have her to thank.

And of course, I would be remiss if I didn't thank the man who made this book possible in the first place—Sir Arthur Conan Doyle, a genius in every sense of the word.

Introduction

Why would anyone want to model his or her life after some-one who never existed?

That may seem like an odd way to start a book titled *Success Secrets of Sherlock Holmes*, but let's face it: Many of you reading this right now are thinking the same thing. And it's all right to be skeptical; Sherlock would certainly approve. After all, at first glance the notion seems rather ridiculous. How could reading stories about a fictional nineteenth-century British detective possibly teach us anything about achieving success in the very different—not to mention very *real*—twenty-first century?

The answer has a lot to do with Sherlock Holmes's creator,

Sir Arthur Conan Doyle (1859–1930), a man who was, by any objective measure, a genius. Born into a large Irish family of respected artists, not only did he invent one of the most famous literary characters in history but he also single-handedly revolutionized the mystery genre itself by introducing fiendishly complex plots that baffled even the most educated readers. In Conan Doyle's hands, the typical whodunit was transformed from a stuffy, predictable piece of fluff into a highly scientific mechanism that unfolded with clockwork-like precision. He was also prolific. In addition to the fifty-six Sherlock Holmes stories and four novels, Conan Doyle wrote more than thirty-five novels and fiction collections in virtually every genre imaginable, from science fiction to the supernatural, as well as a dozen works of nonfiction, including a history of the Boer War in South Africa.

But Conan Doyle was much more than a writer. He was an energetic, idiosyncratic intellectual whose curiosity knew no bounds. A medical doctor by training, he later became one of the first eye doctors in England when the field of ophthalmology emerged in the late nineteenth century. He sought out adventure as well, spending six months on an Arctic whaling ship as a young man and nearly meeting his death in the cold waters near the North Pole. In 1894, he taught himself to ski and was part of the first ski tour across the Alps. Later in life he became obsessed with spiritualism and the unseen world and became one of the world's earliest official ghost hunters, using scientific techniques to study paranormal phenomena (albeit with mixed results). He also tried his hand at real-life detective work, personally investigating two cases of wrongful conviction and saving two men from execution. His efforts exposed the shortcomings of Britain's criminal law system and were partially responsible for the creation of the Court of Criminal Appeal in the early 1900s.

So what does all of this have to do with Sherlock Holmes— and, more importantly, *your* success? The answer is that Conan Doyle funneled a great deal of his real-life genius—and the brilliance of others around him—into Holmes, creating a fictional protagonist greater than the sum of his parts. Likewise, the Holmes stories are much more than mere detective stories. The best Holmes tales operate on two levels simultaneously. For instance, you can choose to read *A Study in Scarlet* as an entertaining adventure tale to pass the time, or you can read it not as a story at all but as a study in genius—as a kind of Victorian-era self-help manual that explains in step-by-step detail how to master your chosen field of study and accomplish the seemingly impossible. Conan Doyle didn't just write superb mysteries, he encoded them with a series of hidden (and sometimes not-so-hidden) clues that can teach us the philosophy and mind-set we need to succeed beyond our wildest dreams—just as he did.

Whether Conan Doyle deliberately added these elements to his stories or if they flowed undetected from his subconscious onto the printed page is an open question (actually, I think it was a little of both, depending on the particular story). But there's no arguing that the *clues are there* just waiting to be uncovered. This book is about helping you identify those clues and convincing you that Conan Doyle's success principles, although more than a century old, are still vital and relevant today.

For just a moment, set aside the conventional image of Sherlock Holmes. Yes, he's witty, intelligent, self-assured, and adventurous—all the qualities any great hero must possess. But think of him in a different way, as a kind of high-quality patchwork quilt—or, better yet, as an avatar, the literary embodiment of the best qualities of the author and his circle of accomplished friends and acquaintances. Conan Doyle moved at the highest levels of British society, and as an educated man, he came into contact with some of the greatest minds of his era. When it came time for him to create a character to star in his mysteries, he couldn't help but borrow a few positive traits from people he knew and incorporate elements of his own personality, too. After all, if you ask a genius to write a story, chances are the final product will contain a little bit of that genius in some way. Julia Child couldn't intentionally cook a bad meal to save her life, and as talented as Michael

Jordan was, he didn't have it in him to purposely play a bad game of basketball. The best can't help but be the best. This is why it makes sense to embark on a close study of Sherlock Holmes: He's a composite fictional character built out of real material. What he did, you can do, too. *Really.*

If you want to understand how something works, you have to take it apart. So in *Success Secrets of Sherlock Holmes*, we're going to break down the Holmes canon the way a master mechanic takes apart a classic hot rod: carefully and with a great deal of respect, mindful of the incredible amount of talent and hard work it took to put it together in the first place. Along the way, we'll make a number of discoveries that not only will completely change the way you look at Sherlock Holmes but will also give you a brand-new set of tools to tackle the challenges and difficulties in your own life. Prepare to give up your preconceived notions about the master detective—and success—for good. Here's a sneak peek:

- **Sherlock Holmes was real.** Some of Holmes's most amazing superpowers—for instance, his ability to size up a person and figure out their entire life history based on a few tiny details—weren't made up at all. As a medical student, Conan Doyle had a professor who used to amaze his students by performing shocking feats of analysis and deductive reasoning. A patient—a total stranger—would walk into the examining room and within seconds, the professor, who had no prior knowledge of the person, began reeling off facts: where the man was from, what he did for a living, his past medical history, and so on (more on this in Secret 4). Conan Doyle never forgot these performances, and when it came time to create Holmes, he essentially created a clone of the professor. This is great news for you and me, because it proves that Holmes's talents aren't unrealistic and out-of-bounds, like Superman's ability to fly or Spider-Man's wall-crawling prowess. If we put in the hard work up front, we too can be just as successful as Holmes.

• **The principles of detection outlined in the Holmes stories are easily adaptable to almost any field of endeavor.** Conan Doyle received a great deal of credit for influencing the development of modern criminology and forensic science. Law enforcement officials were so impressed by the techniques in the Sherlock Holmes stories that they implemented many of them in their own police forces around the world. However, Conan Doyle had no formal law enforcement training. He simply applied the scientific method and diagnostic principles he had learned in medical school to criminal behavior. In the same way, we can take a close look at Holmes's techniques and methods for solving crimes and use them to solve our own real-world challenges, whether it's making an important career choice, grappling with a difficult business or personal decision, or simply trying to make a living doing what you love. The principles are timeless and their real-world applications are endless, regardless of whether you're a student or a stay-at-home mom, a business executive or an orthopedic surgeon . . . or just someone who loves to read mysteries.

- **Many of the principles can be put into practice immediately.** Changing your outlook and becoming more Holmesian in your approach to success doesn't require filling out complicated personality assessments or reading a stack of self-development tomes. In fact, as you'll see shortly, many of Holmes's most famous characteristics—attention to detail, unswerving confidence, laser-like focus—can be learned and applied by just about anyone, regardless of your age or level of education. Each chapter recommends a small, simple way you can tweak a particular attitude or habit for the better.

- **The principles are timeless.** The success principles outlined in this book may have been used by Conan Doyle in his stories, but he by no means invented them. They have been applied over and over again by countless people with their own real-life success stories to tell—and many of them probably never cracked a detective book in their lives. Conan Doyle's great contribution was to gather all of these principles into one bucket—the Sherlock Holmes stories—and let his characters show off their potential within a fictional world.

How to Use This Book

The important thing to point out up front is that *you don't need to have any prior knowledge of Sherlock Holmes to understand or enjoy this book.* Even if you've never read a single Holmes mystery, you'll be able to quickly and easily follow the thread, as each chapter contains copious quotes and plot summaries from the relevant stories. But don't worry. If you plan to read Sherlock Holmes one day—and I hope you'll be inspired to do so—this book reveals the solutions to only a couple of the mysteries. In the meantime, you'll learn a lot about Conan Doyle and the people who influenced his work as well as about Victorian England in general. Consider *Success Secrets of Sherlock Holmes* a hybrid mystery-history-literary-biography-success roadmap.

The book is made up of short, bite-size chapters ranging in length from a few paragraphs to a few pages, and it was designed with all different types of readers in mind. You can read the book from cover to cover, of course. But if you're a natural-born browser, feel free to skip around and choose whichever topics intrigue you the most; almost all of the chapters can be read and understood on their own.

But regardless of *how* you read the book, be sure to keep in mind Holmes's maxim, as expressed in *The Hound of the Baskervilles*: "The world is full of obvious things which nobody by any chance ever observes." The brilliance of Conan Doyle was that he realized achieving success isn't about mastering some obscure skill or tracking down arcane, hard-to-find knowledge. The clues to success are all around us. We just have to learn how to see them.

Sherlock 101

A Few Things to Know Before You Read This Book

If you're already familiar with Sherlock Holmes and Arthur Conan Doyle, feel free to skip this section. However, if you're relatively new to the great detective, here are a few quick facts that will increase your enjoyment of this book:

The first Sherlock Holmes tale, *A Study in Scarlet*, was published in London in 1887. The last collection of Holmes stories was released forty years later, in 1927.

The majority of the stories take place in and around London.

The earliest and most famous Holmes stories were written during the British Victorian era (1837–1901), the period of Queen Victoria's reign. It was a time of great advancements in science and industrialism; Holmes's embrace of the scientific method and his evidence-based, ultra-rational approach to crime solving reflect the zeitgeist of the time.

The Holmes tales were published and often serialized in popular British magazines like the *Strand*. Longer stories were broken up into weekly installments, and impatient fans had no choice but to wait until the next issue appeared on the newsstand to find out what happened next.

In creating Holmes, Conan Doyle was influenced by Edgar Allan Poe's fictional detective, C. Auguste Dupin, who appeared in several mystery stories in the 1840s (including the famous "The Murders in the Rue Morgue" and "The Purloined Letter"), and the French writer Émile Gaboriau's famous sleuth Monsieur Lecoq.

You won't find Holmes's legendary quote, "Elementary, my dear Watson," anywhere in this book. That's because Conan Doyle never wrote it! Nevertheless, over the years it has become part of Sherlock lore. Scholars have traced the origin of the phrase to a comic novel by P. G. Wodehouse, *Psmith, Journalist*, published in 1915; later on it was picked up and used in several of the film adaptations of the Sherlock Holmes stories. Holmes does say "Exactly, my dear Watson" in a few stories . . . still, it's not quite the same.

⋅⊱══◉══⊰⋅

Sherlock Holmes's home and office was located at 221B Baker Street in London. There is a real Baker Street, but no 221B—at the time Conan Doyle invented Holmes, address numbers on Baker Street went up to only 100. However, in 1990 the 221B address was officially given to the Sherlock Holmes Museum. The museum was immediately flooded with letters written to Sherlock from fans all over the world. It received so much mail, in fact, that it appointed a special "secretary to Sherlock Holmes" to manage the postal onslaught and send out form-letter replies.

⋅⊱══◉══⊰⋅

More than a hundred years after his creation, Holmes is still as popular as ever. There are more than 250 active Sherlockian societies and clubs around the world and over one hundred journals, newsletters, and other periodicals devoted to Sherlock Holmes.

"A Passion for Definite and Exact Knowledge"

He appears to have a passion for definite and exact knowledge.
—*A STUDY IN SCARLET*

In the very first Sherlock Holmes story, *A Study in Scarlet* (1887), Arthur Conan Doyle introduced readers to the master detective in a highly unusual manner. When the story begins, John Watson has just been released from the British army after serving in Afghanistan and India. He finds himself in London, desperately in need of a cheap place to live. He happens to run into an old army buddy, Stamford, who works at a local hospital. Luckily, Stamford knows someone who is looking for a roommate to go halves with him on a very nice apartment.

There's just one problem, Stamford tells his friend. This man, a fellow named Sherlock, is a little . . . odd. He works in the hospital's chemical laboratory and spends his days pursuing "out-of-the way knowledge." Stamford tells Watson, "He is a little queer in his ideas—an enthusiast in some branches of science. As far as I know he is a decent fellow enough."

Watson thinks Stamford is holding something back. He presses his old friend to tell him the truth. Stamford hesitates, then says that Holmes "appears to have a passion for definite and exact knowledge." That doesn't sound so bad to Watson— in fact, it seems like a rather admirable quality. But then Stamford finally lets the cat out of the bag. Holmes sometimes takes his passion too far, he tells Watson. In fact, he once caught Holmes in the hospital's dissecting room, beating on human corpses with a stick to see how bruises are formed after death.

That's right: The first mention of Sherlock Holmes in literary history deals with his unfortunate habit of assaulting dead bodies in the morgue. You might think that Conan Doyle threw it in for mere shock value, and it certainly grabs readers' attention. But in fact, he based Holmes's actions on those of a real person: the physician Sir Robert Christison, a towering figure in nineteenth-century medicine who helped shape the curriculum and philosophy of the medical school at the University of Edinburgh, where Conan Doyle studied in the late 1800s. His story can teach us a great deal about the qualities necessary to achieve real and lasting success.

Christison is credited with helping modernize the study of medicine by embracing the scientific method and encouraging rigorous experimentation and exhaustive research in the laboratory. He authored an influential treatise on the effects of poisons and toxins on the human body in 1829 when he was just thirty-two, and went on to write papers on dozens of other maladies, all while serving as a professor at Edinburgh. His dogged pursuit of accuracy and unswerving attention to detail, whether he was dealing with exotic tropical fevers or something as simple as a kidney stone, influenced an entire generation of medical doctors. "You feel that you are in the presence of a mental attitude, and of a kind of investigation, that was entirely different from those of his predecessors; and therefore, that a definite impulse is being given not only to the art, but also to the science, of medicine," his sons wrote after his death in 1882.

Christison was for many years a professor of medical jurisprudence at Edinburgh, specializing in the intersection of medicine and criminal law. He was frequently called on to assist the authorities in solving particularly heinous crimes. One such case was that of Burke and Hare in 1828. The two men were arrested for killing at least seventeen people and selling their bodies to a doctor, who used the corpses to teach his students anatomy. In those days, legally obtained cadavers were very hard to come by, and many doctors resorted to whatever means necessary to get the bodies they needed to teach and continue their research. Unscrupulous men like Burke and Hare were quick to capitalize on the shortage, and began providing black market bodies to physicians for a pretty penny—no questions asked.

Professor Christison was asked to examine the body of one of the victims and determine if the bruises on her body were made before or after death—a crucial question the police had to answer if they hoped to prove murder. The problem was, no one had ever compared premortem and postmortem bruises before. A completely new study was called for, and Christison threw himself at the task with characteristic fervor. He obtained (legally, of course) the bodies of a large dog as well as those of a man and a woman who had recently died, and then set about beating on them with a hammer and heavy stick at regular intervals for several hours (sound familiar?). He made careful notes on the types of bruises that appeared and how they differed from bruises made on living tissue. His analysis was instrumental in finally proving that Burke and Hare were guilty.

At another point in *A Study in Scarlet*, Stamford tells Watson that he wouldn't be surprised to see Holmes take a pinch of poison himself just to understand its effects on the human body. This, too, is a sly reference to Christison, who once famously shocked his colleagues in Edinburgh by taking a large dose of the toxic African calabar bean to experience firsthand its rather unique properties. "Being satisfied that he had taken a dangerous dose of an energetic poison, he swallowed, with characteristic readiness of resource, the shaving-water he had just been using, and thus effectually emptied his stomach," his sons wrote. But it was too late: Christison endured several hours of weakness, giddiness, and muscular paralysis before finally recovering. However, he still got his answer. The good doctor would not be denied—and neither would Conan Doyle: As a medical student, he too experimented on himself, exploring the poisonous effects of the homeopathic herb gelsemium. He took ever larger doses and experienced "some curious physiological results" until a friend finally convinced him to quit. Undeterred, he wrote up his findings, which were eventually published in the *British Medical Journal* in 1879.

The fact that Conan Doyle had Holmes imitate Christison's actions with the cadavers *in his very first story* was no accident. Conan Doyle had obviously been influenced by the master physician's rigorous methods and ferocious tenacity while studying medicine at Edinburgh. Holmes engages in such bizarre behavior in *A Study in Scarlet* for the same reason Christison did in real life—they both had an overriding "passion for definite and exact knowledge." Holmes wants to know *exactly* how a corpse bruises—not because he has a morbid fascination with dead bodies but because it will help him achieve his goal of solving crimes and bringing criminals to justice. Knowing the degree to which bruising can occur on a corpse can help him determine when the blows were administered, corroborate witness testimony, even help identify the murderer. It doesn't matter if other people look at him oddly or whisper behind his back; it's important, and the new knowledge will give him an edge over criminals, so he goes after it, period. No doubt Christison felt the same way. After all, geniuses—both fictional and real—often think alike. Holmes and Christison were single-minded to the extreme. They knew what they wanted and figured out how to get it: by focusing on *every aspect* of their chosen occupations to the point of apparent insanity.

The same is true for your career of choice, whether it's fashion, cartooning, Egyptian archaeology, particle physics, or auto repair. How much do you really know? Are you digging as deeply as you can? Are you living and breathing it? You don't have to put your life on the line like Christison or sneak into morgues like Holmes. It can be as simple as seeking out more experienced professionals in your field—the people who have already made it—and offering to take them to lunch so you can pick their brains. Or do a keyword search at an online bookstore or library website and make a list of every major book written about your field of endeavor, regardless of whether there are five or fifty—then pledge to read them all, no matter how long it takes.

But most importantly, dare to be a little extreme. If your goal is to open a chain of restaurants, then plan a weeklong vacation and visit every single chain restaurant in a hundred-mile radius of your home. Make notes on the menus, the cleanliness of the restrooms, and how many employees are manning the cash registers. Interview the managers and assistant managers. Everyone else might think you're a lunatic for burning a week of valuable vacation time this way, but so what? Remember the image of Sherlock Holmes beating on dead bodies with a stick! There's no such thing as going too far in your determination to be a master in your field.

In *The Sign of Four*, Conan Doyle further illustrates his character's grasp of knowledge during a casual conversation with Watson:

> "My practice has extended recently to the Continent," said Holmes, after a while, filling up his old brier-root pipe. "I was consulted last week by Francois Le Villard, who, as you probably know, has come rather to the front lately in the French detective service. . . .

"He speaks as a pupil to his master," said [Watson].

"Oh, he rates my assistance too highly," said Sherlock Holmes, lightly. "He has considerable gifts himself. He possesses two out of the three qualities necessary for the ideal detective. He has the power of observation and that of deduction. He is only wanting in knowledge; and that may come in time. He is now translating my small works into French."

We often confuse skill with knowledge. In fact, the two are quite different, as Holmes noted in *The Sign of Four*. You can have a great deal of skill in your chosen field, but if you don't back up your skills with knowledge, you'll never truly be a success. And here's the good part: Knowledge isn't that difficult to acquire, especially in the Internet age.

Throughout the Holmes canon, we find several examples of the detective's amazing knowledge of history. I use the word *amazing*, but again, it was simply a matter of his having put in the time and effort to read books and newspapers. If you started running ten miles a day or lifting weights for ten hours a week, the resulting transformation of your body might also be described as amazing by your friends, but in fact, it would simply be the logical outcome of your actions. If you read deeply and intensely in your chosen field, you too will start to amaze people with the storehouse of knowledge you've amassed.

Back in *A Study in Scarlet*, when Watson is first introduced to Holmes by his friend Stamford, Holmes has just discovered a new way of testing for the presence of human blood at a crime scene. Ecstatic, he tells the men how many cases he would have been able to solve had he invented it earlier:

> "There was the case of Von Bischoff at Frankfort last year. He would certainly have been hung had this test been in existence. Then there was Mason of Bradford, and the notorious Muller, and Lefevre of Montpellier, and Samson of New Orleans. I could name a score of cases in which it would have been decisive."
>
> "You seem to be a walking calendar of crime," said Stamford with a laugh. "You might start a paper on those lines. Call it the 'Police News of the Past.'"
>
> "Very interesting reading it might be made, too," remarked Sherlock Holmes.

Remember, though, the point of gaining knowledge isn't simply to impress people at cocktail parties. Holmes knew that his skills at detection would be of little use if he couldn't put them into context. For instance, if he hadn't soaked up the details of so many crimes, he wouldn't have known that a new blood test would be so important. Likewise, his vast knowledge helped him focus his talents on new areas of study—because he had read so widely, he already knew about past discoveries and methods of detection, so he didn't waste his time on reinventing the wheel. He learned from the past and used it to inform his future innovations.

Are You Having Fun Yet?

"Come, Watson, come!" he cried. "The game is afoot. Not a word! Into your clothes and come!"
—"THE ADVENTURE OF THE ABBEY GRANGE"

Imagine you're sound asleep in your warm bed on a frigid winter's night. Other than an emergency like a fire or an earthquake, what could possibly make you get up, throw on some clothes, and venture out into the dark, chilly air?

For Sherlock Holmes in "The Adventure of the Abbey Grange," it was a simple telegram asking for help on a case from a Scotland Yard detective whom he barely knew. Most of us would probably have mumbled a barely audible "No thanks" and returned to blissful slumber. But Holmes's reaction was classic—and extremely telling: He burst into Watson's bedroom with a candle and shook him awake. "Come, Watson, come!" he cried. "The game is afoot. Not a word! Into your clothes and come!" Minutes later they were rattling across London in a carriage, headed for Charing Cross Station to catch a train to Kent and meet the detective at the crime scene. They were in such a hurry, they didn't even stop for breakfast.

Even though "The game is afoot" was actually a quote from Shakespeare's *Henry V*—an allusion some of Conan Doyle's more educated Victorian-era readers no doubt recognized—it quickly entered the pop-culture lexicon and became inextricably linked to Sherlock Holmes. And for good reason; even though Conan Doyle didn't originate the phrase, those four words tell us more about Holmes—and the nature of genius—than almost any other line in the entire Holmes canon.

Look carefully at the quote again: "The game is afoot."

Not "The job is afoot."

Not "The chance to make money is afoot."

Not "Another opportunity to impress Scotland Yard and enhance my reputation is afoot."

Nope. "The game is afoot."

The *game*.

What propelled Sherlock Holmes out of his comfortable bed and into the bitterly cold London night wasn't a chance to pad his bank account, pay the bills, or grab some quick publicity from the London newspapers. Just the opposite! He was racing to meet the detective because it meant a chance to play a game—a game that just so happened to be his livelihood, too. Holmes was ready to have some fun.

If you aspire to be a genius, there's no shortage of advice out there. But before you spend a few years reading self-help books, taking personality tests, and attending three-day seminars on goal setting, take a few minutes to analyze how geniuses act. That's what Conan Doyle did. Having grown up in a family filled with accomplished artists, writers, and thinkers, he developed a unique perspective on how to be successful just by watching how his relatives went about their daily lives. His mother, for example, was a member of Edinburgh's Philosophical Institution and became acquainted with some of the era's most famous intellectuals, including the great physician and writer Oliver Wendell Holmes Sr., whose name the young Arthur would later use for his most famous fictional creation. It's doubtful that he would have ever come up with the idea for Sherlock Holmes in the first place had he grown up in a normal, stable middle-class home. Holmes is a composite sketch of the many geniuses Conan Doyle observed throughout his life; he seems to have taken their best and most powerful qualities and squeezed them all into a single character. It's one more reason why we should pay close attention to the Holmes stories. Conan Doyle is giving us clues to solve a very different type of mystery—how to become a success.

"The Adventure of the Abbey Grange" shows us how a real genius acts. He plays. He has fun. He jumps at the chance to do what he loves, regardless of the time of night (or the temperature). He's an adrenaline junkie. In this respect, Holmes resembles another Brit, the billionaire Richard Branson, the mogul behind the worldwide Virgin brand. He's famous for jumping feetfirst into his diverse business ventures—from magazines to airlines to healthcare clinics—with an infectious sense of enthusiasm. Branson's insistence on having fun has paid off: As of this writing, he's worth well over $4 billion. He's had plenty of successes and many high-profile disasters, but he keeps plugging along with that crazy grin plastered on his face. Why? Because for him, taking huge risks is what it takes to get him out of bed on a cold winter's night.

Geniuses crave these huge risks. In "Abbey Grange," Holmes is disappointed when he and Watson arrive at the scene in Kent and find that the crime—the murder of a local landowner—appears to be rather cut-and-dried, even boring. It's obvious from the testimony of the witnesses that a band of criminals known as the Randall gang broke in and killed Sir Eustace Brackenstall when he walked in on them stealing his valuables. They had also tied up his wife with a cord so they could make a clean getaway. "The keen interest had passed out of Holmes's expressive face, and I knew that with the mystery all the charm of the case had departed," Watson noted. "There still remained an arrest to be effected, but what were these commonplace rogues that he should soil his hands with them?"

For Holmes, being handed a simple mystery was worse than stepping in a pile of dog manure. He craved difficult problems because they forced him to "up his game"; the more difficult the problem, the larger the potential victory, and the greater the sense of satisfaction and accomplishment when he solved it. Luckily, Holmes didn't give up easily. Searching for anything to make the case more interesting, he turned his attention to the crime scene. "Holmes was down on his knees, examining with great attention the knots upon the red cord with which the lady had been secured," Watson tells us. "Then he carefully scrutinized the broken and frayed end where it had snapped off when the burglar had dragged it down."

The frayed cord was the piece of evidence Holmes had been waiting for. By examining how and where the cord was cut, he realized that the story Brackenstall's wife told about the Randall gang couldn't possibly be true. Now he was having fun! The cord led to another piece of evidence, which led to another, until finally he pieced together the truth: Brackenstall had been murdered by a ship's officer who was secretly in love with his wife! Mrs. Brackenstall had made up the whole story about the Randall gang in a futile effort to protect him. In the end, though, Holmes realized that the officer had shown up at the country manor while Brackenstall—a hot-tempered man who had once doused a dog in kerosene and set it afire—was assaulting his wife. The officer had accidentally killed him during the ensuing struggle to protect the woman he loved. In a rare move, Holmes decided not to report his conclusions to the police, and allowed the officer and Mrs. Brackenstall to live happily ever after. He didn't care that the Scotland Yard detective might think less of him for apparently failing to solve the crime, nor was he all that worried about missing out on a nice payday. Like Branson, he wasn't in it just for the money. He had cracked a complicated case; he had satisfied his urge for fun.

You don't become a true genius until you find a way to marry your passion with your career. Real guys like Branson (and fictional ones like Holmes) learned to master the art of oblique goal-setting. Their primary focus was to feed the need inside them. For Branson, it was the rush of competition; for Holmes, intellectual stimulation. In attempting to satisfy that need at all costs—by chasing after their particular definition of excellence, regardless of how weird it seemed to everyone else—they indirectly started attracting other results. In Branson's case, that happened to be billions of dollars. In Holmes's case, it meant developing a reputation as the ultimate master detective. Those are fantastic rewards, but they are mere side effects of their own extremely personal quests for a feeling, a rush, a sense of excitement and accomplishment.

Imagine that it's a cold winter's night. You're buried under a mountain of warm blankets. What could possibly make you race out into the darkness? What could possibly be worth chasing down at this late hour?

The answer will be different for everyone. But *your* answer could literally be worth a fortune.

"An Extraordinary Genius for Minutiae"

"You have an extraordinary genius for minutiae," I remarked.

"I appreciate their importance."

—THE SIGN OF FOUR

Sherlock Holmes is one of the most boring characters in literature.

Think about it. Holmes had very few friends. He spent his evenings brooding in his study or playing his violin (when he wasn't working obsessively through the night, of course). He had difficulty carrying on a casual conversation and didn't keep up with current events. As Watson noted after first meeting and moving in with Holmes in *A Study in Scarlet*, "His ignorance was as remarkable as his knowledge. Of contemporary literature, philosophy and politics he appeared to know next to nothing."

And yet Watson also quickly realized something else about

his new roommate: The guy was a freak for details. Holmes sweated the small stuff, to put it mildly—but only in certain subjects. "Yet his zeal for certain studies was remarkable, and within eccentric limits his knowledge was so extraordinarily ample and minute that his observations have fairly astounded me," Watson observed. "Surely no man would work so hard or attain such precise information unless he had some definite end in view. . . . No man burdens his mind with small matters unless he has some very good reason for doing so."

Watson was soon to discover that some of the most important police detectives in Europe frequently contacted Holmes and asked for his advice on tough cases precisely because he had mastered the nitty-gritty details of his chosen field. Holmes wasn't just a detective; he was a *consulting detective*, an adviser to the professionals. Later, in *The Sign of Four*, the two have this discussion after Holmes reveals he writes scientific papers in his spare time:

"Oh, didn't you know?" [Holmes] cried, laughing. "Yes, I have been guilty of several monographs. They are all upon technical subjects. Here, for example, is one 'Upon the Distinction between the Ashes of the Various Tobaccos.' In it I enumerate a hundred and forty forms of cigar-, cig-arette-, and pipe-tobacco, with colored plates illustrating the difference in the ash. It is a point which is continually turning up in criminal trials, and which is sometimes of supreme importance as a clue. If you can say definitely, for example, that some murder has been done by a man who was smoking an Indian lunkah, it obviously narrows your field of search. To the trained eye there is as much difference between the black ash of a Trichinopoly and the white fluff of bird's-eye as there is between a cabbage and a potato."

"You have an extraordinary genius for minutiae," I remarked.

"I appreciate their importance. Here is my monograph upon the tracing of footsteps, with some remarks upon the uses of plaster of Paris as a preserver of impresses. Here, too, is a curious little work upon the influence of a trade upon the form of the hand, with lithotypes of the hands of slaters, sailors, cork-cutters, compositors, weavers, and diamond-polishers. That is a matter of great practical interest to the scientific detective—especially in cases of unclaimed bodies, or in discovering the antecedents of criminals. But I weary you with my hobby."

Sounds like he'd be a real scream at parties, right? A guy who spends his time analyzing cigarette ashes and staring at pictures of hands is, by definition, boring . . . but also probably very, very good at what he does.

As someone who grew up in a family of accomplished artists, Conan Doyle understood the importance of paying attention to details as a way to become very, very good at what you do. Several of his relatives were prominent illustrators—for example, his father was an accomplished painter and his uncle drew elaborate cartoons and covers for *Punch*, one of the most popular magazines in nineteenth-century Britain. Conan Doyle grew up around men who were constantly perfecting their craft, spending hours to make sure their drawings of famous politicians and London cityscapes were accurate down to the last errant gray hair or tiny cobblestone. Whiling away an afternoon by sketching individual blades of grass for a pastoral scene was monotonous and unglamorous, but for representational artists there was no such thing as a shortcut. Every last detail had to be rendered exactly as it appeared in real life or else the piece was an artistic failure (and no one would buy it, either).

The key to honing the same attention to detail is to first decide exactly what area you want to master. Focus is crucial; you must *specialize*. Deciding that you want to be rich or famous or just a wonderful person isn't enough. Conan Doyle created the character of Holmes, a man who knew he wanted to be a master detective. After that initial decision had been made, figuring out what details to focus on was easy: whatever could help him achieve his goal of being the best in his chosen field. That meant diving deep into the subject matter, much deeper than his peers, the ones who weren't really serious or who just wanted to get by. It meant searching for every scrap of information until he could confidently claim that he knew what other people didn't know—in other words, until he became an expert.

Writing about the Holmes stories in 1898, Thomas Wright said this about the lessons we can learn regarding attention to detail:

> Dr. Doyle's famous character—the prince of minute observers—teaches a great lesson. He is the smart boy . . . grown into a man. How often do we not catch ourselves saying mentally "It doesn't matter." Some even cultivate the habit of being indifferent to everything that goes on around them. Theirs must be a dull life! "Adventures are to the adventurous," says Beaconsfield; and Sterne, in a paragraph that would have served Mr. Holmes as a motto, remarks "What a large volume of adventures may be grasped within this little span of life by him who interests his heart in everything, and who, having eyes to see what time and chance are perpetually holding out to him as he journeyeth on his way, misses nothing that he can fairly lay his hands on." We cannot, we need not wish to be, detec-

tives all of us, but our lives would be much more enjoyable if we would take a leaf out of Mr. Holmes' book and use our eyes.

But Holmes didn't just collect knowledge for the sake of having it; he put his newfound information to work. He was a master at seizing on seemingly insignificant details and using them to construct a person's entire biography. As Holmes explained in *A Study in Scarlet*:

"Before turning to these moral and mental aspects of the matter which present the greatest difficulties, let the enquirer begin by mastering more elementary problems. Let him, on meeting a fellow-mortal, learn at a glance to distinguish the history of the man, and the trade or profession to which he belongs. Puerile as such an exercise may seem, it sharpens the faculties of observation, and teaches one where to look and what to look for. By a man's fingernails, by his coat-sleeve, by his boots, by his trouser-knees, by the callosities of his forefinger and thumb, by his expression, by his shirt-cuffs—by each of these things a man's calling is plainly revealed. That all united should fail to enlighten the competent enquirer in any case is almost inconceivable."

Conan Doyle's most famous technique was to employ the "mountain out of a molehill" routine. He would have Holmes point out a small detail on a person's clothing, for example, and then start riffing. Take the following scene, also from *A Study in Scarlet*. A messenger arrives and delivers a letter to Holmes, who promptly identifies the stranger as a retired sergeant in the Royal Marine Light Infantry:

> Even across the street I could see a great blue anchor tattooed on the back of the fellow's hand. That smacked of the sea. He had a military carriage, however, and regulation side whiskers. There we have the marine. He was a man with some amount of self-importance and a certain air of command. You must have observed the way in which he held his head and swung his cane. A steady, respectable, middle-aged man, too, on the face of him all facts which led me to believe that he had been a sergeant.

It's easy to pass off this sort of thing as an entertaining fictional ploy, a fun way to pull his readers into the story. But Conan based Holmes's technique on an actual person: Joseph Bell, one of his old professors from medical school and a genius in his own right. In an 1892 interview, Conan Doyle recalled his teacher's amazing powers of perception and his ability to apply his knowledge in a practical way:

Sherlock Holmes is the literary embodiment, if I may so express it, of my memory of a professor of medicine at Edinburgh University, who would sit in the patients' waiting-room . . . and diagnose the people as they came in, before even they had opened their mouths. He would tell them their symptoms, he would give them details of their lives, and he would hardly ever make a mistake. "Gentlemen," he would say to us students standing around, "I am not quite sure whether this man is a cork-cutter or a slater. I observe a slight callus, or hardening, on one side of his fore-finger, and a little thickening on the outside of his thumb, and that is a sure sign he is either one or the other." His great faculty of deduction was at times highly dramatic. "Ah!" he would say to another man, "you are a soldier, a non-commissioned officer, and you have served in Bermuda. Now how did I know that, gentlemen? He came into our room without taking his hat off, as he would go into an orderly room. He was a soldier. A slight authoritative air, combined with his age, shows he was an NCO. A slight rash on the forehead tells me he was in Bermuda, and subject to a certain rash known only there." So I got the idea for Sherlock Holmes.

Of course, you can't truly master a subject unless you care about it deeply. Obsession breeds commitment. The only way to survive the hours of tedium necessary to become a genius is to truly love what you're doing.

This type of behavior isn't normal by any means. In fact, in today's society, a great deal of importance is placed on being a well-rounded person who has a broad range of interests. Open up any business magazine and you'll find at least one article devoted to maintaining the work–life balance and how to achieve that mythical state in which you never have to work late, spend plenty of time with your family, and *still* succeed beyond your wildest dreams (yeah, right). Obsession is frowned on. Throwing all of your eggs in one basket and focusing your attention on a single, specialized field to the exclusion of everything else is considered bizarre and unhealthy. But to be the best, you must consciously decide to live an unbalanced life, at least when it comes to your calling. That could mean anything from resisting the urge to indulge in four hours of TV each evening when you could be using that time to sharpen your skills to turning down an invitation for coffee at Starbucks or bowing out of a fun afternoon at the beach to focus on your true passion.

Developing an "extraordinary genius for minutiae" is even more important if you haven't yet found your life's ambition—that single, overpowering, Holmes-esque obsession that pushes you out of bed every morning. You can use the same strategy of focusing on the details to find your niche. Attack any potential calling—be it artistic or corporate—with the same passion as a devotee. Immerse yourself in the experience the same way Holmes dove into his research studies. Remember that Holmes was always the first to admit that he had misinterpreted a particular piece of evidence or had devised a faulty theory to explain a crime. Nevertheless, he continued to examine each potential clue with the same amount of zeal and focus, knowing full well that, more often than not, he would hit a dead end. He accepted the risk and was willing to put in the necessary time—and suffer a few disappointments along the way—to ultimately find the right answer.

Regardless of whether you're living in nineteenth-century London or modern America, you'll never be able to develop that "extraordinary genius for minutiae" if you stick with a career that doesn't interest you. Take the example of Bob Newhart. Before he broke into comedy, the legendary funnyman tried his hand at several different careers. After getting his degree from Loyola University and serving a stint in the army, he got a job as a low-level accountant at a Chicago firm. But, by his own admission, he was a terrible bookkeeper and could never understand why his superiors put such an emphasis on accuracy. His philosophy was, "If you got within a couple bucks, everything was okay."

Needless to say, Newhart didn't last long in the accounting field, and the world—not to mention the company that hired him—is better off for it. It's a humorous story, but it brings up an important point. Newhart didn't succeed because he didn't pursue *accuracy*; he didn't make an effort to master the details and make sure every last penny was accounted for in the ledger books. Why? His heart wasn't in it.

You may have heard the cliché "Good enough for government work." It's a funny line (except, perhaps, if you work in government) and refers to a lackadaisical attitude toward quality. Basically, someone who uses this phrase is saying that there's no need to get it right: "I probably could have done a better job, but it's not as if I'm going to get fired if it's not 100 percent correct, so why bother?" We've all worked with (or for) people who had such an attitude. Like Newhart, their true passion lay elsewhere. They were just going through the motions.

What these folks fail to understand is that there's a direct connection between the little things and the big things. You can't decide to be conscientious only some of the time; excellence doesn't work that way. If you decide to go on a diet and lose twenty pounds, you have to stick with it all day long, day in and day out. You can't make a deal with your stomach to visit the ice cream stand three times a week and ignore the extra calories. You must pay attention to the details of the diet if you want to see the pounds melt away, and you can do that only if you're totally committed to the goal.

Can you imagine someone like Sherlock Holmes ever uttering the phrase "Good enough for government work"? He pursued excellence in everything, be it his day job or playing the violin. What super-achievers like Holmes understand is that paying attention to the details even when it doesn't seem to matter—*especially* when it doesn't seem to matter—is the key to succeeding when the stakes are much, much higher. Why? Because you've had the practice. By focusing on the little stuff and honing your instincts and perfecting your technique, you'll be ready when the big stuff comes along, because the rules for dealing with both are the same. You'll know what to do.

"A Capital Mistake"

It is a capital mistake to theorize before one has data. Insensibly one begins to twist facts to suit theories, instead of theories to suit facts.

—"A SCANDAL IN BOHEMIA"

As a detective, Holmes was aware of the dangers of locking in on a false theory—it could lead you away from the true criminal and, even worse, convince you that an innocent person is actually guilty. Making decisions in your business or personal life without first having a sufficient amount of data can cause serious problems. And if you're intent on succeeding at the highest levels, it can be downright disastrous.

In the 1950s, IBM created the 305 RAMAC—the very first computer with a hard disk drive. The RAMAC was a huge refrigerator-size contraption that ran on vacuum tubes, and the hard disk alone weighed over a ton. Although its capacity was laughably small by today's standards—it could store only about five megabytes worth of data—the RAMAC ushered in the modern era of computing.

George Fuechsel was a technician for IBM and taught programmers how to use the RAMAC. Early on, Fuechsel realized the inherent dangers of relying on a machine for important information. Like Charles Babbage, the nineteenth-century inventor who first came up with the concept of a programmable computer, Fuechsel found that people would quickly put their faith in a hunk of metal and expect it to produce correct information regardless of what was put into it. In fact, Babbage recalled that his customers would often ask him, "Pray, Mr. Babbage, if you put into the machine wrong figures, will the right answers come out?"

To make sure his students didn't make the same mistake, Fuechsel came up with the now-legendary quip "garbage in, garbage out," which was quickly shortened to GIGO. It simply means that if you put bad or incomplete data into a computer, the machine will spew out results that are equally awful and fragmented. You can't expect a machine to turn crappy information into perfect results.

GIGO is true not only in computing but in life as well. Making decisions in your business or personal life without first having a sufficient amount of data—and the right *quality* of data—can cause serious problems. Even though Fuechsel hadn't coined his memorable phrase at the time Conan Doyle was writing, the author understood the importance of quality data and emphasized it throughout his Holmes stories. In fact, he has the master detective repeat a variation of the maxim "Don't theorize before you have all the evidence" at least three times.

In "The Adventure of the Speckled Band," Holmes and Watson are faced with a perplexing mystery: Helen Stoner's young sister has died mysteriously, and her final words were just as perplexing: "Oh, my God! Helen! It was the band! The speckled band!" No one can determine her cause of death, nor do they know what she meant by the "speckled band," although Helen speculated that her sister was referring to a band of itinerant gypsies in the area who often wore spotted scarves around their heads. Were these gypsies somehow responsible for her sister's death? Holmes is baffled until he finally realizes that the "speckled band" was a reference to the last thing she saw before she died—the speckled belly of a deadly swamp adder, the most venomous snake in India. As it turned out, the girls' stepfather, who had spent time in India, was intent on killing them in order to claim their late mother's inheritance for his own. He employed the swamp adder, whose poison is completely undetectable, to kill Helen's sister, and she was next on the list, until Holmes stepped in.

"I had . . . come to an entirely erroneous conclusion which shows, my dear Watson, how dangerous it always is to reason from insufficient data," Holmes said at the end of the tale. "The presence of the gypsies, and the use of the word 'band,' which was used by the poor girl, no doubt, to explain the appearance which she had caught a hurried glimpse of by the light of her match, were sufficient to put me upon an entirely wrong scent."

Eager to solve the case, Holmes had relied on flimsy evidence because he wanted a quick solution: GIGO. Conan Doyle, a savvy observer of human nature, knew that once a person has embraced a certain theory and believes it to be true—regardless of the data he or she used to come to that conclusion—it's extremely difficult to pry that person away from it, even (or especially) in the face of new and conflicting information. Through experiences like this one, Holmes learned not to make a decision or even voice a possible theory about a crime before he had all of the evidence. It was a trait that frequently irritated Watson, who often accused Holmes of being coy. But the detective knew that it was better to keep his mouth shut until he was absolutely sure of the facts.

Feed Your Passion

Our chambers were always full of chemicals and of criminal relics which had a way of wandering into unlikely positions, and of turning up in the butter-dish or in even less desirable places.
—"THE MUSGRAVE RITUAL"

Sherlock Holmes never apologized for being weird. He never tried to justify his numerous eccentricities or defend his decision to become a self-employed detective who worked out of his home—which, in uptight Victorian London, was a rather unusual occupation to say the least.

We have already read about how Holmes beat on cadavers with a stick to understand how bruising occurred after death. In "The Musgrave Ritual," it was revealed that he also liked to pass the time by shooting holes in the wall of 221B Baker Street with a pistol, and stored his tobacco in the toe of a Persian slipper. And in the opening lines of "The Adventure of Black Peter," he surprises Watson early one morning by returning from the butcher's shop with a spear under his arm. He calmly mentions that he had been busy stabbing a dead pig with the spear to work out a theory on how someone might have been killed. Did he try to hide these bizarre actions? Not on your life. In fact, the Holmes adventures abound with examples of the master detective merrily following his muse without giving a second thought to anyone's opinions (including those of his clients). Think of all the time he saved by not having to explain himself! He just went about his business, supremely confident that he was doing the work he was born to do. Nothing was going to stop him.

The legendary science fiction writer Ray Bradbury—award-winning author of countless short stories (one collection is *The Martian Chronicles*) and classic novels like *Fahrenheit 451*—faced a similar challenge when he was a young boy growing up in the 1930s. He loved to collect "Buck Rogers" comic strips from the newspaper every morning, and thrilled at the interstellar exploits of the main character; he was already dreaming of the stars. But his friends started making fun of him. In fact, they razzed him about it so much that one day, desperate to fit in, he ripped his entire collection to shreds. And then promptly burst into tears.

"I started thinking, 'Whose funeral is it?'" he told a reporter years later. "Then I said, 'Fool, it was your future you killed.' If you have a passion, do it. If people doubt you, they are not your friends."

So he went right back to collecting "Buck Rogers" comic strips and jumping headlong into the things he really enjoyed doing—the very things that would build a foundation for his future success. The rest is history.

Conan Doyle wrote almost nothing about Holmes's upbringing, so we're left to guess at how he evolved into a single-minded individual capable of tuning out the sneers and laughter of mainstream society. But perhaps it was as simple as Holmes deciding that he was going to be happy regardless of what anyone said.

Above all else, by focusing on his singular passion and ignoring the opinions of other people, Sherlock Holmes proved that substance wins out over style every single time.

Holmes was a master detective. He achieved this status through an incredible amount of hard work—through obsessing over the details and vacuuming up every bit of relevant knowledge that he could lay his hands on. In the end, he had Scotland Yard at his beck and call. He was the man who could solve the unsolvable crimes. Members of royalty personally visited him to ask for help. As Watson noted in "The Naval Treaty," "To my certain knowledge he has acted on behalf of three of the reigning houses of Europe in very vital matters."

And yet Holmes lived and worked out of a respectable but somewhat shabby little town house on Baker Street. He didn't care about appearances. He had no secretary. He didn't invest a lot of money in nice furniture and the latest fashions. He didn't try to impress his clients with outward displays of wealth and success—but they continued to knock down his door, begging for just a few minutes of his time.

Why? Because in the end, he knew that appearances don't matter—results do.

If you're just starting out, you may be tempted to "fake it till you make it"—to spend lots of money you don't have on the latest tech gadgets, the best clothes, or that awesome apartment you can't really afford. It's a tempting shortcut. But Conan Doyle proved that you don't need a lot of shiny trappings to succeed. He made sure that Holmes used the basic tools of the trade—a magnifying glass, a microscope, chemicals, some basic medical instruments—to work his miracles. Holmes was a genius, but a decidedly blue-collar one. He sweated his way to success.

A couple of bedrooms, a sitting room, some nice windows to let in the morning light. That's all Holmes had, and all he needed.

Your talent is enough. Your passion is enough. Your knowledge is enough.

You are enough.

"A Little Empty Attic"

"You see," [Holmes] explained. "I consider that a man's brain originally is like a little empty attic, and you have to stock it with such furniture as you choose."

—*A STUDY IN SCARLET*

Sometimes, while reading a Sherlock Holmes story, I find that the main character says something so profound that it causes me to momentarily lose track of the plot. I actually have to stop, go back, and reread the passage to make sure I don't forget it. Conan Doyle was a genius at smuggling in bits of his own personal philosophy into his mystery tales. One of my favorite such moments occurs in the very first Holmes–Watson novel, *A Study in Scarlet* (you'll notice that I refer to the novel quite frequently—it has more quotable lines than any other Holmes story in the canon):

"You see," [Holmes] explained. "I consider that a man's brain originally is like a little empty attic, and you have to stock it with such furniture as you choose. A fool takes in all the lumber of every sort that he comes across, so that the knowledge which might be useful to him gets crowded out, or at best is jumbled up with a lot of other things, so that he has a difficulty in laying his hands upon it. Now the skillful workman is very careful indeed as to what he takes into his brain-attic. He will have nothing but the tools which may help him in doing his work, but of these he has a large assortment, and all in the most perfect order. It is a mistake to think that that little room has elastic walls and can distend to any extent. Depend upon it there comes a time when for every addition of knowledge you forget something that you knew before. It is of the highest importance, therefore, not to have useless facts elbowing out the useful ones."

In a nutshell, Holmes is telling Watson that he must be extremely careful about what he chooses to focus on. His point is simple: If you want to be the best at what you do, then you have to be very choosy about how you spend your time. It's actually a rather elegant restatement of the GIGO (garbage in, garbage out) concept that I wrote about in an earlier chapter. Holmes takes it a step further, though, arguing that there is a finite amount of space in our conscious brain. Because there is only so much room in which to place information, we should be extremely careful about what we read, who we spend time with, and even what we listen to on the radio or watch on TV or read on the Internet. I'll leave it to brain surgeons and neuroscientists to argue over whether it's actually possible to fill your brain to capacity; regardless, it's an excellent way to start thinking about . . . well, what you think about all day long. Are you filling your brain with the mental equivalent of junk food or are you stocking it up with healthy organic vegetables from your local farmers' market?

The concept of guarding your mind goes back centuries; it's central to both Buddhist and Christian philosophies. Indeed, the Buddha himself said, "A guarded mind brings happiness." It was also a fundamental part of the success philosophy of the late nineteenth and early twentieth centuries—the same time as the Sherlock Holmes stories were written. In his collection of essays *The Power of Mental Demand and Other Essays* (1916), Herbert Edward Law said the following:

> Make your mind your partner in business. Love your business. Live with it. Feel with it, and make it a beautiful ideal in your mind, and be as careful in shaping everything for its advancement and perfection as you would if you were an artist in making every stroke of the brush add to the element of beauty in the picture. Guard your mind from any

invasion of forces which are opposed to success, which are detrimental to it, which hold it down.

In 1910, Wallace Wattles—who, along with writers like Napoleon Hill (*Think and Grow Rich*) and James Allen (*As a Man Thinketh*), became a self-help superstar—published a book titled *The Science of Getting Rich*, in which he urged readers to consciously decide on the images they allowed into their minds:

> And you cannot hold the mental image which is to make you rich if you fill your mind with pictures of poverty. Do not read books or papers which give circumstantial accounts of the wretchedness of the tenement dwellers, of the horrors of child labor, and so on. Do not read anything which fills your mind with gloomy images of want and suffering.

As you can see, Wattles's advice is very similar to the approach Holmes took to his own work. But before you can guard your mind, you have to first figure out what you're guarding against and what's okay to let in. You need to create a kind of mental bouncer, a muscle-bound gatekeeper who has the ultimate authority over which pieces of information enter your cranial cavity and which ones get turned away. It all ties back into your goals. What are you trying to accomplish? What dream do you hope to bring to fruition? The information aligned with your goals should fill your mind the way metal filings flock to a charged magnet.

The notion of paying close attention to what you allow yourself to think about has gained currency in psychological circles as well. In 1921, Henry Foster Adams, then an associate professor of psychology at the University of Michigan, quoted the "little empty attic" passage in a paper on the power of memory. "While we are in no danger of running out of brain room," he assured us, "this theory, nevertheless, emphasizes the fact that we should limit our memories to those things which are important professionally, socially, politically, and religiously; to those things, namely, which we have occasion and time frequently to review."

More recently, the power to control your thoughts has been recognized as a crucial step in becoming a high achiever. Performance psychologists have realized that one of the reasons elite athletes are so successful in professional sports is because they have trained themselves not to dwell on their past mistakes or shortcomings. In fact, they don't focus a lot of their energy on analysis or evaluation of any kind; they just go out on the field and perform.

Sound like any London detectives you know?

"I Am Glad of All Details"

I am glad of all details . . . whether they seem to you to be relevant or not.

—"THE ADVENTURE OF THE COPPER BEECHES"

As someone who practiced medicine for several years—including a stint in the slums of Birmingham, England—before turning to writing, Arthur Conan Doyle understood the importance of an accurate diagnosis. He knew that to figure out the problem, he had to get all of the facts from his patients. This meant asking about unpleasant and embarrassing physical details they were sometimes reluctant to reveal. But he was also interested in the seemingly irrelevant particulars—the small rash, the mild cough, the chicken that tasted just a bit off—things patients wouldn't even think to mention unless prompted. He knew these boring, apparently meaningless facts oftentimes were directly related to the sickness and, in fact, held the key to a proper diagnosis.

It's no surprise, then, that Sherlock Holmes had a similar attitude toward facts. He wanted all of them, the good, the bad, and the ugly, and regardless of whether his clients thought they were important. Indeed, he would need every scrap of information to solve one of his most perplexing cases, "The Adventure of the Copper Beeches."

His client, Violet Hunter, is a young woman hired as a governess at a very strange country estate called the Copper Beeches. She is offered an amazing salary, but the owner requires that she cut her hair short, wear a blue dress, and spend her evenings in a sitting room with her back turned to a large window. To make matters worse, the child she cares for is a holy terror who tortures small animals, and she is forbidden to enter an entire wing of the large mysterious house. She comes to Holmes and tells him her story, then stops short, saying that certain parts of her tale probably aren't relevant. To which Holmes replies, "I am glad of all details . . . whether they seem to you to be relevant or not."

It's a great line, something only a professional problem solver would think to say. Conan Doyle (and, by extension, Holmes) knew that to figure out what was really going on, it was important to suspend disbelief and judgment and cast as wide a net as possible. Ask for everything. Who knows? The seemingly irrelevant detail may turn out to be extremely relevant later on.

This is a trick every law enforcement officer learns early on. The first step is to gather the facts—*all* of them, not just the interesting or sexy ones. An officer doesn't say, "Just tell me the important facts." That would require the witnesses to immediately evaluate and second-guess their story; they might censor themselves and leave out an important clue because it didn't fit their uninformed definition of what was important.

As it turns out, the frightened governess's attention to detail serves her well. Based on Miss Hunter's story, Holmes eventually discovers the truth: She was hired because of her physical resemblance to the manor owner's daughter, who had just come into a large inheritance from her late mother. Her father demanded that she give him the money, and when she refused, he locked her away in one of the wings of the house. Miss Hunter was hired to sit in front of the window so that his daughter's fiancé would look in from the street and think it was really his betrothed. Because Holmes encouraged her to be completely forthcoming, she had given him everything he needed to solve the case, along with a few irrelevant pieces of information that he easily discarded. Had she left out any one of the odd details—the dress, the hair-cutting, the requirement to sit in front of the window—Holmes might never have solved the case. Separately, each detail made little sense, but together, they formed a mosaic.

If you're trying to solve a big problem, think quantity, not quality. Dig for every available piece of information, even the boring stuff, and don't shy away from uncovering the unpleasant reality of the situation, either. Take a deep breath and ask the uncomfortable questions. Once you have everything, then you can—and should—start separating the wheat from the chaff, the useful from the useless. This second step is crucial; it requires time and careful attention. As Holmes noted in another adventure, "The Reigate Puzzle":

> It is of the highest importance in the art of detection to be able to recognize, out of a number of facts, which are incidental and which vital. Otherwise your energy and attention must be dissipated instead of being concentrated.

A problem—any problem—can be viewed as a kind of crime scene, a set of facts and circumstances waiting to be revealed. Approach each one with the same amount of care as Holmes did, and you'll be surprised at the results.

"Let Us Calmly Define Our Position"

Let us get a firm grip of the very little which we *do* know, so that when fresh facts arise we may be ready to fit them into their places.

—"THE ADVENTURE OF THE DEVIL'S FOOT"

Grace under pressure: Conan Doyle certainly knew a lot about staying calm in desperate circumstances. In 1880, when he was just twenty-one, he signed on for a six-month stint as the surgeon for an Arctic whaling ship. One day when he was out seal hunting on a large ice floe, he slipped and fell into the freezing ocean. No one saw him fall; he was on his own. The edge of the ice floe was too slippery to hold on to, and he began to sink. At the last minute, in what he later described as a "nightmare tug-of-war," he grabbed the hind flippers of the large seal he had just killed and was able to pull himself out of the water, being careful to distribute his weight so as not to pull the seal into the water along with him. His cool, quick thinking had saved his life, and the captain of the ship gave him a new nickname: The Great Northern Diver.

Conan Doyle gave Holmes many of his own surgeon-like qualities: a steady temperament, an unflappable personality, and the innate urge to move toward a problem and solve it rather than run away and find an easier, less-challenging task. Complications are, after all, a surgeon's stock in trade. Throughout the Holmes canon, Conan Doyle provides a unique insight into the mind-set of someone who is tasked with making life-and-death decisions on a daily basis.

If you're facing a difficult problem and you're unsure how to proceed, start by listening to Holmes's advice in "The Adventure of the Devil's Foot." It was one of the master detective's most perplexing cases. While staying with Watson in Cornwall, Holmes is asked to help solve a tantalizing mystery: A woman was found sitting at her kitchen table, dead. Also sitting at the table were her two brothers, who for some unknown reason were babbling and gibbering like maniacs, their faces contorted in terror. They had never before experienced any mental problems and were considered to be upstanding members of the town. Many of the local residents are convinced they were the victims of a supernatural attack.

Holmes investigates, but can find not even the slightest clue of what went wrong. He hits the proverbial brick wall, and so suggests to Watson that they take a walk on the seaside cliffs and search for ancient arrowheads:

> "Now, let us calmly define our position, Watson," he continued as we skirted the cliffs together. "Let us get a firm grip of the very little which we *do* know, so that when fresh facts arise we may be ready to fit them into their places."

Holmes then proceeds to recount the facts of the case as he understands them. He offers a few tentative theories, discards them, then drops the subject altogether. "Meanwhile," he says, "we shall put the case aside until more accurate data are available, and devote the rest of our morning to the pursuit of Neolithic man." In other words: Let's hunt for arrowheads and have a little fun. Watson is amazed. "I may have commented upon my friend's power of mental detachment," he tells the reader, "but never have I wondered at it more than upon that spring morning in Cornwall when for two hours he discoursed upon Celts, arrowheads, and shards, as lightly as if no sinister mystery were waiting for his solution."

When in doubt, chill out. Review, regroup, and refresh. We see this pattern repeated over and over in the Holmes stories. In "Silver Blaze," Holmes says, "At least I have got a grip of the essential facts of the case. I shall enumerate them to you, for nothing clears up a case so much as stating it to another person, and I can hardly expect your cooperation if I do not show you the position from which we start." And in "The Adventure of Wisteria Lodge," he admonishes a flustered client who has just shown up at his door: "Please arrange your thoughts and let me know, in their due sequence, exactly what those events are which have sent you out unbrushed and unkempt, with dress boots and waistcoat buttoned awry, in search of advice and assistance."

Again and again, when faced with a difficult situation, Holmes brings order to chaos and counters emotion with logic. In *The Sign of Four*, he tells Watson:

> "It is of the first importance," he cried, "not to allow your judgment to be biased by personal qualities. A client is to me a mere unit, a factor in a problem. The emotional qualities are antagonistic to clear reasoning. I assure you that the most winning woman I ever knew was hanged for poisoning three little children for their insurance-money, and the most repellent man of my acquaintance is a philanthropist who has spent nearly a quarter of a million upon the London poor."

Another reason why Holmes was so successful is that he wasn't afraid to admit when he was stumped. He never tried to pretend he knew the solution to a hard case and didn't feel the need to constantly act like a genius. He also understood the benefits of unplugging. One of his most famous lines is found in "The Red-Headed League," when, faced with a particularly tough case, he replies, "It is quite a three pipe problem, and I beg that you won't speak to me for fifty minutes." In other words, leave me alone while I puff on my pipe for an hour and just *think*. Holmes was often prone to vegging out, spending hours staring into space or playing his violin, recharging his batteries, allowing his subconscious to work through the minute details of his cases. In fact, Conan Doyle took pains to make clear that it was Holmes's dedication to *relaxation* as well as the science of detection that made him such a success. Take this account of Watson's from "The Red-Headed League":

> In his singular character the dual nature alternately asserted itself, and his extreme exactness and astuteness represented, as I have often thought, the reaction against the poetic and contemplative mood which occasionally predominated in him. The swing of his nature took him from extreme languor to devouring energy; and, as I knew well, he was never so truly formidable as when, for days on end, he had been lounging in his armchair amid his improvisations and his black-letter editions. Then it was that the lust of the chase would suddenly come upon him, and that his

brilliant reasoning power would rise to the level of intuition, until those who were unacquainted with his methods would look askance at him as on a man whose knowledge was not that of other mortals. When I saw him that afternoon so enwrapped in the music at St. James's Hall I felt that an evil time might be coming upon those whom he had set himself to hunt down.

Today, psychologists and performance consultants emphasize the importance of taking breaks, even when you're on a tight deadline. Although it can feel counterintuitive, stepping back and disengaging for a few minutes helps prevent mental fatigue and burnout; it's like pressing the reset button on a computer.

So remember: When you feel your mind start to falter, resist the urge to push on through and squeeze more performance out of your tired brain cells. Instead, create your own tobacco-free version of Holmes's famous pipe-smoking reveries: Go for a short walk, for instance, or send all of your calls to voicemail for a half hour.

Oh, as for those mysterious deaths at Cornwall—well, I don't want to spoil it for you. Read "The Adventure of the Devil's Foot" for yourself and see if you can spot how Holmes applied the principles I outlined here to solve one of his most entertaining (and baffling) mysteries.

The Only Rule Is That There Are No Rules

What one man can invent another can discover.
—"THE ADVENTURE OF THE DANCING MEN"

The next time you get discouraged and think you'll never achieve your goals—or worse yet, that you *can't* achieve them, either because you're not talented enough, don't have the right background, or simply don't have enough money—consider the following:

1. Arthur Conan Doyle, arguably the greatest mystery writer the world has ever known, never took a formal writing course but instead studied medicine and basically taught himself how to write.

2. Despite his distinguished lineage, for many years Conan Doyle lived at or below the poverty level, struggling to make enough money to feed his family.

3. Conan Doyle was never a detective, yet he created the most famous fictional detective of all time. He was never formally trained in criminology, yet Sherlock Holmes's techniques—based on Conan Doyle's experiences in medicine—have influenced generations of real-life detectives and law enforcement officers.

4. Holmes was imperious, sharp-nosed, and thin to the point of being gaunt. As for Conan Doyle, "there was nothing lynx-eyed, nothing 'detective' about him—not even the regulation walk of our modern solver of mysteries," a journalist recalled in 1892. "He is just a happy, genial, homely man; tall, broad-shouldered, with a hand that grips you heartily, and, in its sincerity of welcome, hurts. He is brown and bronzed, for he enters liberally into all outdoor sports—football, tennis, bowls and cricket." In other words, Conan Doyle had very little in common with Holmes either physically or temperamentally, and it didn't matter.

5. Think you can't succeed because you didn't have a great childhood? Consider: Conan Doyle's father was an alcoholic who died in a sanitarium. Two of his sisters died extremely young—one before she was a year old, another when she was just two. His family moved often.

6. Conan Doyle didn't receive any special favors when he decided he wanted to be a writer. He started at the bottom rung, like everyone else, and began writing his stories while still a doctor; he would take a few minutes between patients to scribble down a few lines. When he first started writing, he amassed a collection of rejection letters from all of the major magazines of the day. The first Sherlock Holmes story, the novel-length *A Study in Scarlet*, was turned down by several periodicals before it finally sold to *Beeton's Christmas Annual* for the equivalent of just thirty-eight dollars.

This list of facts may seem a little random, but it points to an important truth: Even Holmes himself couldn't have guessed that someone like Conan Doyle would wind up writing mystery stories, much less create a worldwide phenomenon that is still popular today. In photographs, Conan Doyle looks like just another middle-aged, well-fed Londoner of the late nineteenth century.

There may be a great distance between you and your goals right now. You may not be able to explain in logical terms why or how you're going to succeed. You may feel as if you'll never get there (wherever "there" is for you). And guess what? If a stranger came along and looked at your life, they might agree with you. They might say, "Wow, you say you want to start your own graphic design company, but you're twenty-five years old and still working at McDonald's. Ain't gonna happen!" Or "You want to draw your own comic books? That's insane, you've never even gone to art school."

A stranger could have said the same thing to Arthur Conan Doyle—and who knows? Maybe someone did. But worse yet—what if he had believed them? He might have become just another London doctor, respectable, successful . . . and quite miserable.

Start Small

It has long been an axiom of mine that the little things are infinitely the most important.

—"A CASE OF IDENTITY"

As we have seen, Holmes's awesome displays of deductive reasoning always began with something tiny—a thread, a button, a stain on a piece of paper. He worked from the small to the large, stacking one piece of evidence on top of another. "Let us take it link by link," he advised Watson in "The Adventure of Wisteria Lodge." When he arrived at a crime scene, he would often drop to his knees and zero in on something a room full of Scotland Yard detectives had missed, and inevitably, that would launch him on his way to solving the crime and capturing the murderer. He was never looking for the major clue or the big score; he was content with starting small.

We can see this principle at work in the opening pages of

countless Holmes stories when he first meets his clients: Invariably he ushers them into his sitting room and urges them to tell their story in great detail from the very beginning. Oftentimes it's frustrating for the reader, because Conan Doyle presents us with so many seemingly minor pieces of information before we finally get to the good stuff. But as is usually the case, he's a few steps ahead of us. For instance, in "A Case of Identity," Miss Mary Sutherland wants Holmes to help her find her missing lover. She embarks on a long, meandering tale that seems to be about everything but the problem at hand. At one point, Watson muses, "I had expected to see Sherlock Holmes impatient under this rambling and inconsequential narrative, but, on the contrary, he had listened with the greatest concentration of attention." Indeed, Holmes encourages her to tell him even more about her life, at one point exclaiming, "You interest me extremely." And of course, in the end, those seemingly trifling details are the key to unlocking the whereabouts of her boyfriend.

There are numerous advantages to following Holmes's link-by-link approach. For one thing, there's almost no pressure. Small tasks are, by their very nature, relatively easy to accomplish. This is one reason Holmes always had a leg up over the official police; unlike them, he wasn't interested in solving the crime as quickly as possible to take all the credit, get his name in the papers, or earn the praise of his superiors.

When those are your priorities, the pressure to get fast results often leads to sloppy analysis and overlooked clues. But instead of walking into a room and asking himself, "Who killed the victim?" Holmes instead asked, "What can the room tell me about the events that took place here?" He didn't go hunting for big game right away. Instead, he started breaking down the crime scene into pieces—the rug, the chair, the murder weapon—each of which he could sift through for clues.

We can adopt the same attitude in chasing down our own life goals. You've probably heard the old saying, "Inch by inch it's a cinch, but mile by mile it takes a while." Today business and life consultants still teach the same principle, albeit in more modern language; they urge their clients to break down big tasks into small chunks to make them more manageable and avoid stressful "freak-outs."

In fact, an entire management philosophy has sprung up around this idea. The Work Breakdown Structure (WBS), first pioneered by the U.S. Department of Defense in the 1950s, is a formalized method of breaking down large tasks into small chunks. It's essentially an organizational chart on steroids, by which huge projects are taken apart and segmented until each individual component is identified and assigned to a particular person or division for completion. It's the only way the government can get a handle on incredibly complex jobs like building a new aircraft carrier or implementing a new software system.

Scotland Yard relied on Holmes so frequently because its detectives allowed themselves to become overwhelmed by the enormous task facing them: Who committed this impossible crime? How will we ever catch them? How could this happen? They saw the forest but forgot that it was made up of individual trees. Don't make the same mistake. Instead, attack your giant tasks like Sherlock did—one piece at a time.

"A Trade of My Own"

Well, I have a trade of my own. I suppose I am the only one in the world. I'm a consulting detective, if you can understand what that is. Here in London we have lots of government detectives and lots of private ones. When those fellows are at fault, they come to me, and I manage to put them on the right scent. They lay all the evidence before me, and I am generally able, by the help of my knowledge of the history of crime, to set them straight.

—*A STUDY IN SCARLET*

Have you ever wondered why Sherlock Holmes never joined Scotland Yard and became a detective? Let's face it: With his track record, he could have been running the entire operation in a matter of months. But he had other ideas. He didn't want to be tied down with a nine-to-five job (can you imagine supervising him?). He much preferred working out of his home, setting his own schedule, and creating his own job opportunities. Holmes was a great detective, but he was an even greater entrepreneur.

Holmes created an entirely new career for himself, one that had never existed before. Conan Doyle did the same thing, hopping from medicine to ophthalmology before settling into writing. But he wasn't just an ordinary writer—he made a very comfortable living by becoming one of the first writers to create a character (Holmes) who starred in a recurring series of unconnected stories. Up until then, most writers either wrote stand-alone stories (with a beginning, middle, and end contained in one piece) or magazine serials (long, episodic series that ended in a cliffhanger each week, enticing the reader to buy the next issue to find out what happened next).

But Conan Doyle had an idea: Why not create a character who shows up in stories over and over again, but the stories are each self-contained mysteries? It was the best of both worlds, combining the stand-alone genre with the serial, and it was an instant success. Victorian-era London simply couldn't get enough of the strange new detective.

Flip around the cable channels and you'll see more examples of people making good livings (sometimes *very* good livings) doing jobs that you won't find listed in any how-to-choose-a-career manual. Take the History Channel's *American Pickers*, for instance: Two guys drive around the country picking through other people's junk (literally) in search of collectible treasures. They buy rusty cans, old auto parts, and broken bicycles, then refurbish and resell them to collectors, often making a big profit in the process. And then there's the

Discovery Channel's *Dirty Jobs*. Creator and host Mike Rowe has become a multimillionaire by shining a spotlight on grubby, smelly entrepreneurs who pay the bills by . . . well, you name it: cleaning roadkill, raising worms, removing chewing gum from sidewalks, recycling sludge—even collecting owl vomit.

Yes, owl vomit.

This is not meant as a clarion call to abandon your nine-to-five job and set off on some quirky odyssey. Many people (myself included) find that their nine-to-fives not only pay the bills but also provide a great deal of fun and purpose in their lives. But there is a fount of variety even within the traditional corporate world and many different ways to spend those eight hours. Your particular talents may push you in a direction you never thought you'd go. The key is knowing that, like Sherlock Holmes, you too can make a living as a one-of-a-kind . . . *whatever.*

Approach Problems with a Blank Mind

> We approached the case, you remember, with an absolutely blank mind, which is always an advantage. We had formed no theories. We were simply there to observe and to draw inferences from our observations.
>
> —"THE ADVENTURE OF THE CARDBOARD BOX"

Predictable football teams rarely win championships because their opponents can easily figure out their game plan. Directors who make predictable movies with clichéd plots don't often win Academy Awards because everyone knows how the movie will end five minutes after it starts. Every day we're told that to succeed in business, sports, or the arts, we have to be *un*predictable—original, unique, daring. It's true. But here's the paradox: The key to being original and unique is to implement a predictable, methodical strategy to achieve our goals.

One of the main reasons Sherlock Holmes was so successful was that he always approached problems in the same way. He came to each case with a blank, or open, mind—that is, he came to the case with no preconceived notions, no hunch as to who was guilty or not guilty, no predilection toward a certain kind of outcome. Indeed, Holmes enjoyed uncertainty and surprise. He was never happier than when a case suddenly took a dramatic turn and pulled him into unknown territory.

Holmes's blank-mind approach was no doubt influenced by Conan Doyle's rigorous medical training at the University of Edinburgh, where the scientific method was paramount. As one early-twentieth-century scientist put it, "The scientific method insists that the student approach a problem with open mind, that he accept the facts as they really exist, that he be satisfied with no half-way solution, and that, having found the truth, he follow it whithersoever it leads."

Conan Doyle made sure that Holmes adhered rigorously to the scientific method, so much so that his stories, while entertaining, are somewhat predictable in their structure. Over and over again he used this systematic approach, like pressing a cookie cutter into fresh dough. Check out the stories yourself and see if you can spot the pattern:

1. The client is welcomed into Holmes's office and asked to recite the facts as clearly as he or she can.

2. Holmes listens intently, interrupting only to ask a clarifying question. He makes very few editorial comments or judgments about the client.

3. When the client is finished, Holmes makes a decision about whether to take the case based on the facts presented (luckily for the reader, he almost always takes the case).

In other words, mysteries are presented to Holmes in much the same way that medical cases were presented to Conan Doyle the physician. Like a doctor, Holmes does not pass judgment on his "patients," regardless of what they might have done to put themselves in their present predicament. What good would judging them do? It would only antagonize them and make them less likely to cooperate. The important thing is to focus on the facts so that the proper remedy can be applied.

Before pilots fly their planes, they must walk around them and complete a preflight check, a routine set of inspections. The preflight check never changes. It's a consistent way of making sure everything's in working order before the plane ever leaves the ground. Holmes was smart enough to realize that to succeed as an unconventional entrepreneur (the world's only consulting detective), he needed a similar solid, well-thought-out plan of action. Ironically, his methodical, step-by-step approach gave him the firm foundation from which he could improvise and test out his radical new ideas about solving crimes. Regardless of how "out there" he got when tracking down a murderer, he never strayed from the boundaries of his preestablished plan.

Preparing yourself to deal with a problem is often the most important part of the problem-solving process. Don't wade into the middle of something until you've adopted a Holmesian sense of detachment and objectivity. Walk in with an open mind, and you'll be ready to start filling it with facts, not emotions.

Be Wary of Complexity

Perhaps, when a man has special knowledge and special powers like my own, it rather encourages him to seek a complex
explanation when a simpler one is at hand.

—"THE ADVENTURE OF THE ABBEY GRANGE"

Although he was a genius, Sherlock Holmes wasn't perfect.
Conan Doyle was careful to give his detective some all-too-
human flaws that made the character more believable and
multidimensional. In the end, though, Holmes's recognition
of his own flaws helped him become more self-aware and, by
extension, a better detective.

Holmes craved challenges. He wasn't interested in making
an easy buck—in fact, easy cases bored him to tears. In "The
Adventure of the Abbey Grange," Watson said that sending
Holmes out on a simple case was like sending a highly trained
medical specialist to diagnose a case of common measles. And

in "The Adventure of the Priory School," he made special note of Holmes's "love of the complex and the unusual."

But this desire for difficult cases could also cause problems. In "Abbey Grange," Holmes told a Scotland Yard detective, "Perhaps, when a man has special knowledge and special powers like my own, it rather encourages him to seek a complex explanation when a simpler one is at hand." In other words, sometimes the solution to a problem might be rather simple, but since he enjoys difficult cases, he might subconsciously avoid that simple solution to feed his constant need for challenges. Holmes was smart enough to occasionally take a step back, evaluate his actions, and make sure he wasn't falling into traps of his own devising.

Although we might not want to admit it, many of us—especially those who have a lot of experience in a certain field—have the same problem as Holmes. When faced with a difficult situation, we often come up with overly complex solutions and shy away from simple fixes. Why? Sometimes it's just plain ego: "I'm smart, therefore I should come up with an ingenious and unique solution that no one has ever thought of before." Unfortunately, *ingenious and unique* often translates into "needlessly complex" and "almost impossible to understand."

At other times, we veer toward the complex solution because we simply want to impress someone else. If your supervisor gives you a task to complete, you have an opportunity to prove your worth to the company and separate yourself from the pack. What better way to do that than whip up a thirty-minute PowerPoint presentation, complete with a dozen charts and graphs? Or if someone asks you for advice, rather than give him a simple answer, you drone on for fifteen minutes so he knows how well-informed you are.

Some of the greatest minds in engineering and software have faced similar temptations over the years. Clarence "Kelly" Johnson, the legendary aircraft engineer who headed up the Lockheed Skunk Works program, which produced dozens of high-tech, top-secret planes for the U.S. military, is perhaps best known for coming up with the KISS Principle, which stands for "Keep it simple, stupid." That simple four-word phrase was the guiding principle behind the creation of some of the world's most advanced flight and weapons systems. The idea was to keep the design of the plane as simple, efficient, and practical as possible so that when something went wrong, it could be found and fixed quickly and easily.

However, valuing the simple over the complex isn't a new idea; it goes back centuries. In fact, the most famous Holmes quote of all from *The Sign of Four*—"How often have I said to you that when you have eliminated the impossible whatever remains, *however improbable*, must be the truth?"—hearkens back to this idea. If you're having trouble implementing your success strategy, or don't feel that you're getting any closer to your ultimate goal, it might be a good idea to evaluate your methods. Is your game plan too complicated? Are you trying to do too much too soon? Are you overanalyzing what it takes to achieve the results you want?

Experienced salespeople—even those who sell complex, high-dollar products like software systems or robotic arms—learn how to boil down the essence of their offerings into what's known as an "elevator pitch." The idea is to come up with a simple, quick, and accurate description of the product you're selling, a pitch that you can complete in the span of a short elevator ride with a prospective client. This forces you to focus on the core value that the product provides and what sets it apart from the competition. The elevator pitch is KISS in action. Holmes would certainly approve!

Death to Modesty

> "My dear Watson," said [Holmes], "I cannot agree with those who rank modesty among the virtues. To the logician all things should be seen exactly as they are, and to underestimate one's self is as much a departure from truth as to exaggerate one's own powers."
>
> —"THE ADVENTURE OF THE GREEK INTERPRETER"

No one ever accused Sherlock Holmes of being modest, much less someone who lacked confidence. At times his attitude was interpreted as rude, cocky, and even arrogant. But in reality, Holmes was simply being honest. He was the best, he knew it, and he saw no reason to hide the fact; it would be illogical to do so.

Modesty would also have been devastating to Holmes's business. Remember, he wasn't just any old private detective; he was a *consulting* detective. Other professionals and members of Scotland Yard came to him when they were stumped. What good would it have done for him to adopt an "Aw shucks, it was nothing" attitude? He was extraordinary, and to pay the bills, he had to let word get around. He wasn't going to let a false sense of humility stand in the way and block his success.

Excessive modesty will get you nowhere. In fact, it can be just as damaging as excessive arrogance. If you keep downplaying your achievements and telling people, "It's no big deal," sooner or later they'll start to believe you. At the same time, you don't want to walk around like a proud peacock, alienating your friends and building a reputation as a world-class jerk. So what's the solution? What's the difference between arrogance and confidence?

In his best-selling collection of dialogues *The Art of Happiness*, the Dalai Lama addresses that very question. He distinguishes between two types of ego—one that focuses on selfish desires and another that focuses on service to others. "In order to fulfill that wish to be of service, one needs a strong sense of self, and a sense of self-confidence. This kind of self-confidence is the kind that leads to positive consequences."

The Dalai Lama's explanation of positive self-confidence is one we see illustrated in the character of Holmes. Although his manner could sometimes be abrasive, for the most part the detective knew how to communicate his excellence in a way that didn't sabotage his career. He didn't walk up to his clients and say, "I'm the best." Instead, he *demonstrated* his abilities on the spot—usually through his now-famous habit of telling clients their life story after sizing them up for only a few seconds and seizing on the tiniest detail of their appearance. Holmes was constantly performing, showing people that he could back up his confident words with actions. But he also knew when to stop talking and get to work.

Holmes also rarely displayed his prodigious skills for purely egotistical purposes; he didn't go out of his way to humiliate people or shame them with his superior intellect. Displaying his talent to new clients was a way of convincing them he was the right man for the job.

Nor did Holmes ever claim to know something that he didn't actually know. His extreme self-confidence was always genuine and rooted in real knowledge. In other words, he was prepared. He knew he had done his homework, both literally and figuratively—remember the analysis of the 140 different types of tobacco ash?

Everything Is Useful

"Data! Data! Data!" he cried impatiently. "I can't make bricks without clay."

—"THE ADVENTURE OF THE COPPER BEECHES"

City birds are tough. I discovered this fact when I moved to Washington, DC, in the mid-1990s after spending most of my life in rural Arkansas. My mother collected birds' nests, and I was very familiar with the types of nests that country birds created: all-natural, symmetrical, aesthetically pleasing. But after a few months in the city, I realized that urban birds had an entirely different approach to nest building. Whereas my country birds worked only with organic materials—straw, grass, leaves, flowers—DC birds didn't have that luxury. They lived in a world of asphalt, pollution, traffic jams, and huge concrete buildings, so when it came to building nests, the big-city birds improvised. They used trash. Lots and lots of trash.

Do you know the number one building material preferred by urban birds? Those long, thin, jagged strips of cardboard that you tear off to open packages sent by overnight courier companies. They are perfect insulation for nests, and they're strong enough to provide reinforcement to the entire structure. One strip is long enough to wind around the entire length of a good-size nest; it's the equivalent of a steel girder in a modern office building. In DC and other large cities, you'll find dozens of these strips in gutters because people anxious to get at whatever's inside that box simply rip 'em, toss 'em, and forget 'em. For birds, finding one of those strips is like stumbling across a brand-new twenty-dollar bill.

One man's trash is another bird's treasure. More than treasure, actually—it constitutes a huge part of the bird's life. Without that trash, nests couldn't be built in the city, bird homes couldn't be established, and little city birds couldn't be born. In fact, from the bird's point of view, there's no such thing as trash, just resources waiting to be utilized.

When it comes to the creative process, we can learn a lot from those city birds. Inspiration can come from anywhere; you don't need a password or special permission to access it. The raw materials for creating art—be it a painting, story, poem, or song—are all around us. If you don't believe me, just take a look at Arthur Conan Doyle's body of work.

The Sherlock Holmes stories, universally recognized as some of the greatest mystery stories ever written in any language, are literary patchwork quilts, Frankenstein monsters made up of hundreds of pieces of Conan Doyle's life. Virtually every Holmes story has at least one or two details that Conan Doyle plucked from his own experiences. He took ordinary reality and molded it into extraordinary fiction.

We've already seen how the character of Sherlock Holmes was inspired by two of his professors in medical school, Dr. Joseph Bell and Sir Robert Christison. In a letter to Conan Doyle in 1893, friend and fellow writer Robert Louis Stevenson complimented Conan Doyle on his "very ingenious and very interesting adventures of Sherlock Holmes," but added, "Only the one thing troubles me: can this be my old friend Joe Bell?" The character's very name was also a product of Conan Doyle's upbringing: "Sherlock" was the surname of a school chum from childhood, and many scholars believe "Holmes" was a reference to his mother's friend, the American physician and intellectual Oliver Wendell Holmes Sr. ("Never have I so known and loved a man whom I have never seen," he wrote.) As a teenager, Conan Doyle was sent to a Scottish boarding school, Stonyhurst, where he met a pair of brothers named Moriarty, later appropriated as the name of Holmes's greatest rival. A chance meeting with a newspaper reporter on an ocean voyage who later charmed Conan Doyle with ghostly tales of Devonshire, the brooding area of England where the journalist had grown up, sparked the idea for Conan Doyle's most famous Holmes story, *The Hound of the Baskervilles*.

Conan Doyle didn't rest on his laurels, waiting for inspiration to strike him—he realized early on that it surrounded him at all times. All he had to do was reach out and take what he needed, like plucking a piece of fruit from a tree. If you find yourself stuck, lacking inspiration for your artistic endeavors, remember that Conan Doyle created literary gold out of common details. In and of themselves, each piece didn't amount to much—a borrowed name here, an old recollection there—but once assembled into a whole, their power was unmistakable. Conan Doyle used the same principle in building his plots: Holmes solved seemingly impossible mysteries by focusing on ordinary, everyday details that everyone else overlooked.

Maybe the next great idea for a product or service won't be discovered at an expensive business seminar, but in the streets of your very own neighborhood, by focusing on the simple, unglamorous problems facing local businessmen. The painter Edward Hopper didn't have to travel to faraway European locales to find arresting subjects for his art; he found them on the very "ordinary" streets of New York City. Everyone else ignored the middle-class people on their way to work and the half-empty cafés on street corners, but not Hopper. He learned to see—*really* see—what was right in front of his nose, and found enough drama and human complexity to rival any play by Shakespeare. The result was a series of classic American paintings like "Nighthawks." So think about it. Could your inspiration be hiding behind the ordinary details of your own life?

Find the Right Watson

Good old Watson! You are the one fixed point in a changing age.
—"HIS LAST BOW"

Pity poor Watson. Of all the characters in literature, he is perhaps the most misunderstood and misrepresented. Over the years, through endless pop-culture incarnations of the Sherlock Holmes mysteries on radio, television, and in the movies, Watson has been reduced to a buffoon, a clownish character who follows Holmes around like a lost dog. Every time Holmes discovers a clue or makes an observation, Watson is right there to spit out his pipe and exclaim wide-eyed, "Impossible!" or "Blimey! However did you solve it, Holmes?"

But in fact, the Watson of Conan Doyle's original stories

is a very different character: a solid, intelligent war veteran with steely nerves and a strong sense of honor and loyalty to Holmes. As Watson tells us himself in the very first Holmes story, *A Study in Scarlet*, he served with the British Army in Afghanistan after receiving his medical degree and was seriously wounded in the battle of Maiwand; the bullet "shattered the bone and grazed the subclavian artery" in his shoulder. "I should have fallen into the hands of the murderous Ghazis had it not been for the devotion and courage shown by Murray, my orderly, who threw me across a packhorse, and succeeded in bringing me safely to the British lines," Watson recalled.

Not exactly a dimwitted old fool, to say the least! *London Times* columnist Ben Macintyre also believes that Watson has gotten short shrift over the years. In 2009 he wrote a column in praise of the doctor, highlighting the contrast between the two characters' personalities. "Holmes is flashy, brilliant and extraordinary," he writes, "but it is Watson's blunter, quieter virtues of simple decency that we are called on to admire, and it is his voice that we trust. . . . Watson is the man you would want to go into the jungle with or, for that matter, into the Afghan mountains."

Although Holmes gets most of the glory, Watson was nevertheless a significant factor in the detective's success. He was in many ways the perfect junior partner and friendly companion for the prickly genius; the two complemented one another quite well. The actor Jeremy Brett, who memorably played Holmes on a BBC TV series in the 1980s, once noted in an interview, "Watson and Holmes are two halves of the same person. They are Sir Arthur Conan Doyle . . . you can't have the one without the other, it's impossible."

If your plans for success require you to work closely with someone else for a long period of time, you could do a lot worse than Watson. Let's look at some of the qualities that made him such a valued business partner:

- **Watson had parallel skills and training.** It makes sense that Conan Doyle, himself a physician, would make Watson a doctor as well. Holmes, too, was quite skilled in medicine and chemistry, especially poisons (of course!). This meant that the two had something in common; they could speak the same language. Holmes wasn't a certified doctor like Watson, and Watson wasn't a freewheeling detective like Holmes, but their knowledge and experience overlapped enough to provide them with a comfortable rapport.

- **Watson was independent.** Watson didn't *need* Holmes; he had a successful medical practice and a life of his own.

Shortly after moving to London, he married and settled down, and sometimes months would go by between his visits with the famous detective. It wasn't a master–servant relationship; Watson didn't need Holmes's approval to maintain his own sense of self-worth, nor did he show up at 221B Baker Street every morning desperate to win Holmes's praises. It was a healthy and mutually agreeable partnership, and Watson eventually earned Holmes's greatest respect.

- **Watson was a good sounding board and knew how to listen.** Earlier, I quoted a passage from "Silver Blaze" in which Holmes tells Watson the facts of the case as a means of getting a clearer picture of the situation. And in "The Boscombe Valley Mystery," Holmes says, "Look here Watson . . . just sit down in this chair and let me preach to you for a little. I don't know quite what to do, and I should value your advice. Light a cigar and let me expound."

- **Watson wasn't afraid to challenge Holmes and make him think harder.** Watson spent a lot of time on cases asking Holmes questions and demanding that he explain himself. This was good for Holmes, whose antisocial tendencies sometimes made him almost impossible to work with. By constantly engaging him and not allowing him to curl back into his intellectual shell, Watson helped humanize Holmes.

- **Watson didn't try to take Holmes's place.** Over time, Watson came to understand that the best way he could serve Holmes—and, by extension, help solve cases—was not to try to compete with him but to allow the detective to do what he did best and then assist Holmes by using the special talents and skills that he himself brought to the table.

- **Watson believed in Holmes's work.** This might seem to be an obvious point, but in many partnerships, one person is in it for ideals, while the other is just out to make a quick buck or steady paycheck. Successful long-term partnerships need emotional and intellectual buy-in from both parties. As the chronicler of Holmes's amazing adventures and the person entrusted with portraying the detective to a large audience, Watson believed he was performing an important service, not just for law enforcement but for society in general.

Success is never a one-person job. Regardless of how independent you are (or *think* you are), you'll still need help along the way. Finding the right partners to help you reach your goals is just as crucial as securing funding from a venture capitalist or putting the finishing touches on your first novel; the quality of feedback you receive is as important as the product or service you ultimately provide. Watson was a fictional character, but his virtues are very real—always be on the lookout for them.

How to Be a Good Watson

> I swear that another day shall not have passed before I have
> done all that man can do to reach the heart of the mystery.
> —WATSON, IN *THE HOUND OF THE BASKERVILLES*

We have just seen the important qualities to look for in a good long-term partner who can support your efforts. But what if you're the prospective partner—in other words, what if you're a Watson working for a Holmes? How can you leverage the relationship to not only help *your* Holmes succeed but also achieve your own goals as well?

Let's go over a few more qualities you'll need to become the perfect Watson:

1. **Have a genuine interest in your partner's work.** You can't be supportive of someone else's dreams if you don't believe in them or, worse yet, find them boring. Watson was in-

trigued by Holmes's occupation, and he got a real thrill out of helping him solve cases. Watson's own medical background also came in handy from time to time. Although he wasn't as devoted to crime solving as Holmes, it was fulfilling enough to keep him coming back for more.

2. **Don't want what your partner has.** If you're the junior partner, so to speak, it helps if your goals are different from the other person. If you want to *be* that other person— have all of his or her talent and power—then your role as a supportive partner is shaky to say the least. Jealousy can begin to creep in to the relationship, and you might find yourself subconsciously undermining your partner to show that you, in fact, have what it takes to be Holmes. The key is to want to succeed on your own terms and to recognize the benefits of being the second-in-command: What can you learn from your position that will help you achieve your own unique goals?

3. **Have other interests outside of your work.** In other words, have a life. Watson was married and had a successful medical practice. Whereas Holmes put all of his eggs in one basket and combined his life with his work, Watson, as the junior partner in the enterprise, maintained a healthy distance. This stance—having one foot in the real world and one foot in the adventurous world of Holmes—kept Wat-

son grounded. He was able to play devil's advocate and view Holmes's theories through the prism of practicality and common sense.

4. **Challenge your Holmes for the right reasons.** One of Watson's most admirable qualities was that he never grew envious and embittered over Holmes's incredible talent. When he challenged one of Holmes's assumptions or questioned his modus operandi, he did so out of a genuine sense of concern (or just plain curiosity), not ego. Like Holmes, Watson had an insatiable thirst for knowledge.

5. **Use your talents to fill gaps in the partnership.** If you want to succeed as a right-hand man, you will need to do an honest inventory—not only of your own skills and shortcomings but of your Holmes's strengths and weaknesses, too. You probably already have a good idea of what you do well and not so well. Now, how can your talents complement your partner's? No one's perfect, after all. Holmes was a genius, but he was also overly rational and emotionally cold, often devoid of almost any human feeling. Watson recognized this and used his own compassionate and generous nature as a counterbalance.

It's not easy being a good Watson, but learning to be a supportive partner is important. At one time or another in our lives, most of us will have to serve in an apprentice role, either to learn a new skill or simply to assist someone else do an important job. And by learning what it takes to help another person succeed, we'll be better able to choose our own Watson down the road when the roles are reversed.

The Fun Stuff Comes at the End

Patience, my friend, patience!

—A STUDY IN SCARLET

My friend was irritated. We'd been browsing the aisles of a used bookstore one day when I came across an old paperback copy of Sherlock Holmes stories. When he said he'd never read any before, I convinced him to buy it. "You'll love them," I promised. But when we met up a couple of weeks later and I asked him about it, he rolled his eyes.

"I thought this Sherlock Holmes guy was supposed to be the hero of the stories," he said.

"Well, he is," I replied.

"Then why does he just sit around so long and wait?"

I told my friend I had no idea what he was talking about.

"Well," he said, "I read the first five or six stories, and

every time, Sherlock just sits there for the first half of the story. He doesn't do anything. The client comes in and tells him about some problem, and he just . . . sits there. The only real fun stuff comes at the end."

"What do you mean by fun stuff?" I asked.

"You know," he said, shrugging. "When he actually goes out and solves the crime or catches the murderer or whatever. Those are the good parts. Why do we have to wait so long for the good parts?"

My friend's complaint isn't just limited to mystery stories. Most of us are impatient; we'd like to fast-forward through the boring parts of life to get to the moments of real fun and rewards. When I was a little kid, I became hooked on Godzilla movies, which often played on our local television station. This was in the days before VCRs, though, so I had no choice but to sit through the setup portion of the movie, when the plot was laid out and the main (human) heroes were introduced. This was pure torture for me. I wanted to see monsters smashing Tokyo. I didn't care about a bunch of Japanese scientists and their cute assistants.

After the conversation with my friend, I went back and skimmed through some of the Holmes stories. Looking at it from my friend's perspective, I realized he was right: There wasn't a lot of action in the first two thirds of any given story. And yes, Holmes did spend an awful lot of time sitting in his parlor listening to other people talk. In fact, in many of the stories' opening sections, Holmes doesn't even seem to be the main character—the spotlight is given over to his clients or to Scotland Yard detectives who describe the crime that has just occurred. The "fun stuff," as my friend put it—Holmes springing into action, analyzing crime scenes and solving the mystery—comes much later.

Here's the catch, though: The Sherlock Holmes mysteries wouldn't be nearly as exciting or mind-boggling if it weren't for those inactive beginnings when seemingly nothing happens. In fact, an awful lot is happening. When Holmes sits and listens to his clients, he is absorbing all of the information and concentrating on nothing else but the case at hand. He has to understand the situation before deciding on his course of action. That means keeping his mouth shut and listening.

The same is true for almost anything worthwhile. You have to put in a certain amount of work up front—boring, seemingly inconsequential work at times—before you can begin to reap the rewards.

As a doctor, Conan Doyle knew the importance of listening to his patients before he was able to make an accurate diagnosis. He transferred that same quality of patience and attentiveness to Holmes, a character who loved adventure and adrenaline-pumping chases as much as anyone—but who also knew that to experience those thrills, he had to put in the time up front.

In today's fast-paced entertainment culture, we rarely need to wait for anything. You can order movies on demand through your cable system or download them from the Internet in twenty minutes. And if you don't want to spend two hours watching the whole thing, you can log on to a video site and search for clips of the best scenes—or better yet, just find the movie's website or fan site and read the entire plot summary in less than a minute. After a while, we begin to believe that we'll achieve success the same way—instantly, by skipping over the boring parts in the beginning and leapfrogging past the intermediate stages; we'll just create our future, as if we were manipulating a photo, until it looks the way we want it to look.

But we know, deep down, that we can't live our entire lives pointing and clicking. For the past year or so, a construction company has been erecting a large hotel next to my apartment building. The vacant lot they chose to build on was nothing but a deep ravine clogged with weeds and vines. A team of workers cleared out the underbrush and then began building supporting walls to shore up the soil surrounding the site. Concrete had to be poured, a parking garage had to be dug, and the hotel's electrical and plumbing systems had to be hooked into the city's underground utility lines. It was slow, hard work, and oftentimes it appeared chaotic: Building materials were scattered everywhere, and at any given moment carpenters and electricians were working on a half-dozen different projects. The days dragged on, and it didn't seem as if they were making any progress whatsoever. But then, almost overnight (or so it seemed), the entire structure of the multistory hotel was put into place: floors, steel girders, drywall, and windows. It had taken a long time to prepare the foundation, but once it was completed, the rest of the project—the fun stuff—took off like a rocket.

If you're just starting on a big project or are still toiling in the early stages of your career, at times it can seem as if nothing is happening—that you're working and working but making no visible progress. Don't get discouraged. The bigger your dream, the higher your goals, and the more time and preparation you'll need to devote to it. It can seem like a mystery at times, and mysteries are, by their very nature, incomprehensible—until they're solved, of course. Then suddenly everything falls into place, and it all makes perfect sense, just like watching that hotel being built.

In the Sherlock Holmes stories, no matter how complicated the plot becomes, we never really get that upset, because we know that, in the end, Holmes will figure it all out; the suspense is momentary and enjoyable. In real life, of course, there are no guaranteed solutions to our problems, no master detective is rushing to our aid, and *suspense* is just another word for "stress." Nevertheless, it helps to remember that problems often come veiled in an illusion of impenetrability. "I'll never figure this out!" we think. But Conan Doyle, an experienced physician who had dealt with many perplexing diagnoses, knew that persistence is often the key to unraveling even the knottiest conundrum. It's no coincidence that Holmes never gave in to despair—he was always the one bucking up Watson and convincing his partner that the solution was just around the corner.

The Holmes stories give us the luxury of pacing. We're introduced to the main characters, then we proceed to the crime scene, then watch as Holmes works his magic. It's all very orderly and sequential. In the real world, however, it doesn't work that way. Oftentimes we're dumped into the middle of a problem without the benefit of any orientation session. During those stressful times, remember Holmes's entreaty in *The Sign of Four*: "It clears every instant. I only require a few missing links to have an entirely connected case." Rather than focus on the chaos, focus on the fact that you have the ability to bring order out of that chaos. And remember—the fun stuff always comes at the end.

Give Away Your Secrets

It has always been my habit to hide none of my methods, either from my friend Watson or from any one who might take an intelligent interest in them.

—"THE REIGATE PUZZLE"

When you think about it, the idea sounds crazy: To beat the competition and become the best in your field, go around and tell everyone all of your trade secrets. And hey, why not try to teach other people how to do what you do, too?

That's exactly what Sherlock Holmes did. He happily gave away his secrets and always thoroughly explained how he solved each and every case. He sometimes pretended to feel otherwise—in *A Study in Scarlet*, for instance, after Watson asks him a question about the case, he jokingly replies, "You know a conjurer gets no credit when once he has explained his trick; and if I show you too much of my method of working, you will come to the conclusion that I am a very ordinary individual after all."

But in fact, Conan Doyle was careful to paint Holmes as someone who had no interest in maintaining an air of mystery; his love of knowledge was equal to his desire to spread that same knowledge. He became Watson's de facto instructor in the Holmesian method of detection, constantly encouraging his sidekick to get involved and try his hand at solving a case or, at the very least, analyzing a few clues. In "A Case of Identity," after the duo are visited by a woman searching for her missing stepfather, Holmes asks Watson, "Now, what did you gather from that woman's appearance? Describe it." Watson gives him a detailed description, down to the color of the beads on her jacket. "'Pon my word, Watson, you are coming along wonderfully," Holmes replies.

But why would Holmes try to train Watson in his methods? After all, they more or less "belonged" to Holmes—he created them, and he used them to solve his cases and maintain his livelihood. Why run the risk of showing everyone else how to do it? Wasn't he just asking for more competition?

Actually, no—he was behaving very shrewdly (did you expect anything less from Holmes?). He knew that by training Watson he was keeping him motivated. Holmes could be a terribly annoying companion, and he caused the doctor a great deal of grief. Revealing his methods was a form of payback—a way to show Watson that he trusted him. Also, he knew that Watson wanted to be treated as a part of the team and that he genuinely enjoyed learning new things and developing a new set of skills.

Second, by giving away his trade secrets, Holmes might have been trying to take some of the pressure off of himself and make life a little easier. Rather than just have Watson come along for the ride, he wanted to put him to work—if he could train him, that meant Watson could actually help Holmes solve cases more quickly. A second, trained set of eyes never hurts.

When you're working with other people on a project, make an effort to share the intellectual wealth. Your partners no doubt have the same levels of ambition, pride, and need for mental stimulation as you do. Motivate them by letting them in on the method to your madness. Why do you do the things you do? What are you trying to accomplish? How can they help you (and, by extension, the entire group) reach those goals?

Holmes could have made fun of Watson's lack of knowledge. He could have constantly scorned him for not being able to keep up with his own rapid-fire intellect. But he didn't. He made sure Watson had a chance to learn and grow; Holmes knew that by empowering his friend he would, in the end, reap even greater rewards.

Have Friends in Low Places

I found that [Holmes] had many acquaintances, and those in the most different classes of society.

—*A STUDY IN SCARLET*

Sherlock Holmes had an incredible intellect and razor-keen instincts; his clients included members of the highest echelons of London society, and if anyone deserves the label *elite*, it's Holmes. However, he wouldn't have been nearly as successful if it hadn't been for a ragtag group of street urchins known as the Baker Street Irregulars. These dirty, uncouth kids regularly supplied Holmes with the street-level information he needed to solve crimes. He called them "the Baker Street division of the detective police force," and he was only half-joking. "There's more work to be got out of one of those little beggars than out of a dozen of the force," Holmes remarked in *A Study in Scarlet*. "The mere sight of an official-looking person seals men's lips. These youngsters, however, go everywhere and hear everything. They are as sharp as needles, too; all they want is organization."

A few years later, in *The Sign of Four*, Holmes again calls for the help of the Irregulars to track down some vital information, and again tells Watson that they "can go everywhere, see everything, overhear everyone."

Holmes, of course, could have spent his time hobnobbing with royalty or sipping brandy with the head of Scotland Yard. But he knew the importance of hanging on to his friendships with the lower classes. He knew how helpful they could be and realized that to be a success—the best detective in all of England, if not the world—he needed every possible edge he could get.

When we learn to disable our mental judgment switch and stop saying no to people based on their outward appearance, a whole new world of opportunities opens up. By focusing on the quality of the case rather than the quality of the client's outfit (or his or her ability to pay), Holmes was able to hone his skills on some of the most challenging mysteries London had to offer—poor people, it seems, get into just as much trouble as the rich. As he solved each successive mystery, his reputation grew, which in turn attracted more clients, some with very deep pockets. So in the end, Holmes's willingness to say yes to London's lower classes wound up benefiting him not just professionally and artistically but financially as well.

His relationship with the Irregulars also underscores the point that Holmes was smart enough to realize his limitations. He was a tough guy, no doubt about it, but as an expert in many fields himself, he understood the importance of relying on experts in other areas where he wasn't as proficient. The Irregulars certainly qualified as experts in the rough-and-tumble world of the London peasant class.

Unfortunately, too many successful people don't follow Holmes's example. As soon as they get that big promotion and fancy title, they have little use for the secretaries, mailroom attendants, and junior-level interns who work on the lower floors. They'd much rather spend their time schmoozing with the boss or squeezing in a round of golf with their buddies on a Friday afternoon. The same is true in social settings, as well: At one time or another, we've all met someone who evaluates people based on the number of zeros in their bank account. If you drive a BMW and wear Gucci, they're all smiles—but they barely notice the clerk at the grocery store, and don't think twice about treating the neighborhood babysitter like an indentured servant.

This birds-of-a-feather mentality can backfire, though. Any senior executive worth his or her salt will tell you that it pays to be nice to people on the way up the ladder, because you may find yourself saying hello to them on the way down as well. And inevitably, a day will come when Ms. Power Suit is late for a meeting and desperately needs help from the Lowly Ones to put together a report. Will they jump to her aid, or take their own sweet time (or pretend they can't find the stapler)?

Keeping the lines of communication open between everyone, not just a select few, can reap other dividends, too. The CEO may call the shots, but the CEO's secretary is the true power broker. The modern-day Baker Street Irregulars of the corporate world are the gatekeepers; they decide which calls get forwarded to voicemail and which e-mails mysteriously find their way into the junk folder. The same principle holds true outside the office—treating the person behind the desk at the DMV with respect is not only the right thing to do, but can also get you out the door a lot quicker! Taking the time to cultivate all of life's relationships—the big and the little—can reap great rewards down the line.

Honor Your Teachers

Education never ends, Watson. It is a series of lessons with the greatest for the last.

—"THE ADVENTURE OF THE RED CIRCLE"

In previous chapters we've seen how Conan Doyle was influenced by two teachers in medical school, Sir Robert Christison and Joseph Bell, and how he ultimately paid tribute to them by incorporating elements of their personalities into the character of Sherlock Holmes. Although he did not pursue a lifelong career in medicine, Conan Doyle was deeply grateful for having had the opportunity to sit at the feet of such towering figures. By immortalizing them in his fiction—and openly acknowledging their influence in countless interviews—he was demonstrating to his mentors how much they meant to him.

Much of the self-development movement these days is

about looking to the future, focusing on your goals and leaving the past behind. *Potential* is the new buzzword. But Conan Doyle understood that to be a success, he had to learn from the people who had walked the path before him, whether in medicine or fiction (before he began writing mysteries, Conan Doyle devoured every contemporary detective story he could find).

Roman Emperor Marcus Aurelius, who became emperor in 161 CE, wrote the now-classic *Meditations*. His work has influenced countless generations, and one of the most striking aspects of the book is how it begins. Rather than immediately begin to lay out his own philosophy of life or recount his own victories and accomplishments, Marcus Aurelius does something quite amazing: In a book that is dedicated to understanding the meaning of life, he first looks backward, not forward.

1. From my grandfather Verus [I learned] good morals and the government of my temper.

2. From the reputation and remembrance of my father, modesty and a manly character.

3. From my mother, piety and beneficence, and abstinence, not only from evil deeds, but even from evil thoughts;

and further simplicity in my way of living, far removed from the habits of the rich.

4. From my great-grandfather, not to have frequented public schools, and to have had good teachers at home, and to know that on such things a man should spend liberally.

One of the greatest works of literature in history begins with what amounts to a laundry list of what Aurelius has learned from people older and wiser than himself. It's a stunning display of humility and reveals Aurelius's own great wisdom, too. The emperor doesn't shy away from the hard lessons, either; a little later he writes that from a man named Rusticus "I received the impression that my character required improvement and discipline."

Lasting success is built not only on achievements but on lessons learned. Conan Doyle created one of the most unique and popular characters in literature because he had watched and listened to his own old masters, like Christison and Bell. What have you learned from the important people in your life? Have you taken the time to list the qualities you admire in yourself that can be traced back to someone else? The sooner you realize that it's not all about you, and that your success depends just as much on the positive influence of others as on your own hard work, the more willing you'll be to accept criticism and listen to a little friendly advice from people who've traveled the same path you've chosen.

Mimic the Method

[Holmes] was able, by the exercise of his sense organs and his
reasoning faculties on some concrete object, to construct a
whole chain of facts with which that object was connected.

—E. A. LAMBORN

It's difficult for modern audiences to understand the influence
Sherlock Holmes's method of detection had on late nine-
teenth- and early twentieth-century society. The character
was a phenomenon; virtually every educated person in London and America followed his exploits from the late 1800s
until well after World War I ended in 1917. Professionals
from all walks of life realized that, although they were reading fiction, the principles laid out in the stories nonethe-
less had enormous practical value. An anonymous reviewer
writing in *The Critic* in 1892 summed up Holmes's method
this way:

This man [Holmes] does not belong to Scotland Yard or to any other organized band of men who follow his profession. He works alone and with such success that his reputation becomes national, and mysteries, the solution of which has completely baffled other men, are placed in his hands with perfect confidence as to their ultimate unraveling. His methods are simple, logical and curiously interesting. When the subject upon which he is to work is laid before him he thinks it all out and makes up his mind as to the solution and where it may be sought. Then he begins to build upon his theory, closely observing the smallest details of each circumstance as it appears, seizing eagerly upon this one and promptly rejecting that until his theories become facts and the chain of evidence is welded to his satisfaction. A worn side to a shoe, an unexpected opening of a window, a knot in a bundle tied in a peculiar manner, or some other item equally insignificant will give him the necessary clue and make his work a simple process.

Professionals in various fields took that Holmesian method seriously and began applying it to some of the thorniest problems of the day. In 1905, for instance, the scholar E. A. Lamborn proposed using the Sherlock Holmes method to teach elementary-school children and develop their logical faculties more quickly. He broke the method down into four major parts, using the plot of "The Adventure of the Blue Carbuncle" and one of its major characters, Henry Baker, as an example.

The first part of the method was careful *observation*. Lamborn gave the example of how, in the story, Holmes "was able, by the exercise of his sense organs and his reasoning faculties on some concrete object, to construct a whole chain of facts with which that object was connected." He pointed out how the detective took a rather common object—a man's hat, belonging to Baker—and examined it extremely closely, observing, in Lamborn's words, "the size, shape, condition, kind of lining, newly-cut grizzled hairs, smell of lime-cream, tallow stains," and so on.

With these external facts in hand, Holmes moved on to the second part of the method, *deduction*. By analyzing the facts associated with Baker's hat, he was able to deduce, even before meeting Baker, that due to its high quality but slightly shabby condition, he had once been quite well-off, but had recently fallen on hard times.

Then, Lamborn said, it was on to stage three, as Holmes used the *memory* of past experiences to help him fill in even more details. "For example, his memory informed him that the particular shape he had observed was in fashion three years before, so fixing the time of the hat's purchase," the educator wrote. The final piece to Holmes's method was *con-*

structive imagination, defined by Lamborn as the detective's ability "to combine his facts and build them into a homogenous hypothesis—that the person he wished to discover was Henry Baker, a man formerly well-to-do, fallen on evil days, of sedentary habit, in poor domestic circumstances, etc."

Another real-life example of the Holmes method in action can be found in the *British Medical Journal* from 1900. An eye doctor decided to apply Holmes's principles to his own practice, with remarkable results:

> In another case the patient was a nurse-maid, aged from 16 to 17, who came with a little boy, aged from 12 to 14 months, in her arms. She was suffering from trachoma, which had become acutely inflamed. . . . Dr. Van Duyse at once forbade her carrying the child, and she promised to obey. When she returned two days later, however, the surgeon on seeing her frowned and said in a severe tone: "In spite of my prohibition you have been carrying the child. I shall be obliged to let your master and mistress know what is the matter with you." The girl stoutly denied that she had been carrying the child, but Dr. Van Duyse insisted that hardly twenty minutes before she had been carrying it on her right arm, and had handed it over to someone else at the door. The girl, amazed at the almost supernatural insight of the surgeon, confessed her transgression.

Here, too, there was nothing more occult than a recent tell-tale trickle of urine running obliquely from right to left across the girl's apron. The art of observation may be cultivated by attention to such apparent trifles . . . the method of Sherlock Holmes is a powerful aid to success in treatment.

The Holmes method can even be applied to sales. At the height of Holmes's popularity, in 1915, master salesman Harlan Read wrote in his training manual *Read's Salesmanship*, "A perusal of any of the Sherlock Holmes stories will interest the salesman in the quality of observation which the salesman must cultivate. Sherlock Holmes had a remarkable faculty for finding out what sort of people he was dealing with, through powers of close observation. The author, Conan Doyle, takes pains to explain in every story that Sherlock Holmes did nothing by chance, and did not rely upon any invisible, peculiar or mystic power to aid him in making his deductions. He had simply cultivated a shrewdness of observation. This is a quality that the salesman must cultivate. It will enable him to understand his customer."

Education, sales, real-life law enforcement . . . the Holmes method is applicable to almost any field of endeavor, antiquated or modern.

Picture Your Dreams
As Reality

One of the quaintest proofs of Holmes's reality to many people is that I have frequently received autograph books by post, asking me to procure his signature.

—SIR ARTHUR CONAN DOYLE

In 1917, Conan Doyle wrote an article for the *Strand Magazine* reminiscing about the creation of his greatest character, Sherlock Holmes. In the essay, he confesses that he was astonished to realize how many of his fans thought Holmes actually existed. The character was so dynamic and well-written that he literally leapt off the magazine page and into the physical world, at least in the minds of some readers:

One of the quaintest proofs of Holmes's reality to many people is that I have frequently received autograph books by post, asking me to procure his signature. When it was announced that he was retiring from practice and intended to keep bees on the South Downs I had several letters offering to help him in his project. Two of them lie before me as I write. One says: "Will Mr. Sherlock Holmes require a housekeeper for his country cottage at Christmas? I know someone who loves a quiet country life, and bees especially—an old-fashioned, quiet woman." The other, which is addressed to Holmes himself, says: "I see by some of the morning papers that you are about to retire and take up bee-keeping. If correct I shall be pleased to render you service by giving any advice you may require. I trust you will read this letter in the same spirit in which it is written, for I make this offer in return for many pleasant hours." Many other letters have reached me in which I have been implored to put my correspondents in touch with Mr. Holmes, in order that he might elucidate some point in their private affairs.

Of course, Holmes wasn't the only fictional character who has seemed to take on a life of his own. Walter B. Hudson (writing under the pen name Maxwell Grant) was a prolific pulp writer in the 1930s who created the famous crime-fighting character The Shadow. Hudson concentrated intensely on his work, and wrote most of the three hundred–plus Shadow novels at his apartment in Greenwich Village, New York. Legend has it that after he died, subsequent residents of the apartment reported being haunted by a large figure that looked eerily similar to The Shadow. Experts in the paranormal speculated that Hudson may have concentrated on his character so much that he inadvertently created a tulpa, a mystical creature that originates from a person's focused thoughts and willpower.

Well, you don't have to believe in tulpas to understand how powerful fiction can be (after all, you're reading this book!). Conan Doyle and Hudson were both able to create larger-than-life characters that transcended the printed page because of their vivid imaginations and ability to see them as three-dimensional people. Holmes is a fully rounded character, not a cardboard superhero stereotype; he's brilliant, but he's also moody, emotionally damaged, and a frequent user of cocaine. His voice is as unique today as it was in 1887; even if you've never read a Sherlock Holmes story, you know him on some level.

Your challenge is to invest the same amount of imagination and creativity in your goals as Conan Doyle invested in writing Sherlock Holmes. It's important that you have clear, detailed, and extremely specific goals—give each one its own personality. If it's a tangible goal, picture it in your mind until you can feel, taste, and hear it. Imagine the heft of it in your hand. If the goal is more intangible—say, a promotion at work—imagine what you'll feel like when you achieve it. Even if you're not the creative type, you can still paint by numbers, right? Imagine your goal as a black-and-white outline. Fill in the empty shapes with vivid colors until it's so bright it hurts your eyes. Before long, you'll start believing that what you want is already real—and it's closer than you think.

Rebel at Stagnation

I cannot live without brain-work. What else is there to live for?
—*THE SIGN OF FOUR*

Restlessness, the desire to constantly tackle new challenges, an inability to give in to laziness . . . these are all qualities found in exceptional individuals, from Michael Jordan and Donald Trump to (you guessed it) Arthur Conan Doyle and Sherlock Holmes. Winners always seek tougher challenges and hunger for new opportunities.

Take Conan Doyle, for instance. In 1890, at the age of thirty-one and with a wife and new baby daughter to support—and having already found success with his first few Sherlock Holmes stories—he gave up a comfortable career in general medicine and plunged headlong into something he found to be an even bigger challenge: the then-new field of eye surgery and ophthalmology. He moved his family from England to Vienna and, later, Paris to study, then moved back to London and opened up a new practice. All the while he continued to write at a furious rate. While buried deep in his optometry studies, he managed to knock out a thirty-thousand-word short novel, *The Doings of Raffles Haw*, along with the first draft of a much longer historical novel and numerous short stories.

Like all geniuses, Conan Doyle's intellectual restlessness never abated. In addition to medicine and detective writing, his other passions included spiritualism and contacting the dead; at one point he even investigated the possible existence of fairies. Shortly after the first Holmes stories were published, he decided to spend the next two years meticulously researching life in fourteenth-century England under the reign of Edward III in preparation for a novel, because he believed the time period had never been adequately covered by a writer. When asked in 1892 why he undertook such a massive task, he replied simply, "I determined to test my own powers to the utmost."

Small wonder, then, that Sherlock Holmes was also a restless spirit (to say the least). For Holmes, boredom equaled death. You might even go so far as to call him an adrenaline junkie. In *The Sign of Four*, Holmes tells Watson:

"My mind," he said, "rebels at stagnation. Give me problems, give me work, give me the most abstruse cryptogram, or the most intricate analysis, and I am in my own proper atmosphere. . . . But I abhor the dull routine of existence. I crave for mental exaltation. That is why I have chosen my own particular profession, or rather created it, for I am the only one in the world."

That last sentence is important. Holmes's need for intellectual stimulation was so great that when it couldn't be satisfied through regular means—getting a nine-to-five job, for instance, and living a mainstream life—he had to take matters into his own hands. He created his own reality.

Years later, in "The Adventure of Wisteria Lodge," Watson and Holmes are eating lunch one afternoon during a lull between cases, when Holmes says:

"My dear Watson, you know how bored I have been since we locked up Colonel Carruthers. My mind is like a racing engine, tearing itself to pieces because it is not connected up with the work for which it was built. Life is commonplace; the papers are sterile; audacity and romance seem to have passed forever from the criminal world. Can you ask me, then, whether I am ready to look into any new problem, however trivial it may prove?"

The lesson is clear: If you want to achieve something re-markable, you must align your mind with "the work for which it was built." As we've seen over and over again, Holmes knew exactly what made him happy and what gave his life purpose; armed with that knowledge, he was able to direct all of his energies in pursuit of those goals.

If you already know what you were born to do, then pur-sue it with the same energy as Holmes pursued his cases—but be prepared to do double-duty and put in long hours, as Conan Doyle did; chances are you won't be able to quit your day job right away.

But what if you have no earthly clue about what you should do with your life? Simple: Keep looking until you find some-thing that ignites in you the same fire and passion that Holmes had for detection. Conduct a personal inventory of your skills and talents and then try to match them to a complementary career. Just because you weren't born with a passion doesn't mean you can't find one. But whatever you do, keep moving forward. Remember Holmes's words: *Rebel at stagnation*. Don't allow your inner engine to stall out. When you find your-self starting to obsess over a particular career path or field of study, when you begin daydreaming about the possibilities and turn off the TV to read more about it, then you'll know that you've tapped into your inner Holmes.

One of the most fascinating aspects of Holmes is how

closely his words and actions track with the techniques advo-
cated by the leading self-improvement thinkers of the day.
The similarities are so striking, in fact, that one can't help but
wonder if Conan Doyle was familiar with their works. Take
Orison Swett Marden, for instance. Marden was a popular
speaker and author around the turn of the twentieth century
who encouraged his audiences to break out of their narrow
confines and strive for greatness. In 1894 he wrote a book
titled *Pushing to the Front*. As you read the following quotations from the book, ask yourself if they remind you of a
certain British detective:

> You have not found your place until all your faculties are
> roused, and your whole nature consents and approves of
> the work you are doing; not until you are so enthusiastic in
> it that you take it to bed with you.

> As love is the only excuse for marriage, and the only thing
> which will carry one safely through the troubles and vex-
> ations of married life, so love for an occupation is the only
> thing which will carry one safely and surely through the
> troubles which overwhelm ninety-five out of every one
> hundred who choose the life of a merchant, and very many
> in every other career.

Follow your bent. You cannot long fight successfully against your aspirations. Parents, friends, or misfortune may stifle and suppress the longings of the heart, by compelling you to perform unwelcome tasks; but, like a volcano, the inner fire will burst the crusts which confine it and pour forth its pent-up genius in eloquence, in song, in art, or in some favorite industry.

Fired up yet? One final caveat: Success won't necessarily come easily or quickly. Conan Doyle toiled for many years as both a doctor *and* a writer—"medicine in the day, sometimes a little writing at night," he recalled—before he was able to quit medicine and devote all of his time to his stories and novels. He wrote dozens of stories before creating the character of Holmes, and many of them were sold to magazines for just a few dollars . . . but he *persisted.*

Remember Norbury

Watson . . . if it should ever strike you that I am getting a little overconfident in my powers, or giving less pains to a case than it deserves, kindly whisper "Norbury" in my ear, and I shall be infinitely obliged to you.

—"THE YELLOW FACE"

Holmes balanced his extreme sense of self-confidence with a healthy dose of humility. He was smart enough to know that even though he was brilliant, that didn't mean he would always make the right decision.

In "The Yellow Face," published in the *Strand Magazine* in 1893, Conan Doyle gave Holmes his biggest challenge to date: failure. Holmes and Watson are visited by Grant Munro, who lives in Norbury, a small village just outside of London. His wife, Effie, is behaving mysteriously; he believes she is having an affair but has no proof, even though he spies a mysterious masked figure in a nearby cottage she visits regularly. When Holmes learns that she had been married once before, in America, he quickly decides that the mysterious figure is actually her first husband, even though she claimed he had died of yellow fever. It seems obvious enough (to him, anyway) until the masked figure is caught and turns out to be Effie's young daughter. Effie confesses: Her first husband really is dead, but he had been a black man; thus her daughter is of mixed race. She kept the existence of the child from her second husband because she was afraid he would disown her for once having been married to a minority. In fact, though, Grant Munro "lifted the little child, kissed her, and then, still carrying her, he held his other hand out to his wife and turned towards the door."

The story is famous for not only tackling the prickly subject of interracial marriage (it was 1893, remember), but also taking a strong stand against conventional racist attitudes in Britain. Holmes and Watson are delighted to see the family united and happy, but on the carriage ride home from Norbury, Holmes tells Watson to be on the guard against the detective's overconfidence in the future. *Norbury* will be their secret code word, a warning that Holmes is perhaps letting his ego decide the outcome of a case rather than relying on his tried-and-true methods of logic and deduction.

Holmes didn't obsess over his mistakes (see Secret 6), but he didn't ignore them, either. He knew there was always a lesson to be learned from analyzing what went wrong; overconfidence can be just as disastrous as coming up with the wrong solution to a mystery. It's important that we take the same approach in our lives. You know yourself better than anyone; what are your shortcomings, the little tricks of ego that trip you up time and again? Once you've identified the problem areas—your own personal Norburys—you can be on your guard against them (and more importantly . . . so can everyone else!).

Talent Isn't Enough

If the art of the detective began and ended in reasoning from an arm-chair, my brother would be the greatest criminal agent that ever lived. But he has no ambition and no energy.

—"THE GREEK INTERPRETER"

Perhaps the most interesting character in the entire Sherlock Holmes canon appeared only a handful of times: his older brother, Mycroft. Very little is known about Mycroft, but the few details Conan Doyle gives us paint an interesting—and valuable—portrait.

In "The Greek Interpreter," Watson and Holmes are relaxing on a warm summer evening after tea when the discussion turns to the nature-versus-nurture debate: If someone is gifted in a particular area, is it due to heredity or their training? Watson's opinion is that Holmes's knack for observation and deduction are due to his extensive training. Holmes says that's true "to some extent," but argues that heredity plays a large role as well, and claims his brother is an even better detective than he.

That's right. Mycroft was even more intelligent than Sherlock—no small feat! Watson, like the rest of us, is shocked by the revelation. He can't understand why, if Mycroft is so smart, no one has ever heard of him. Holmes replies:

"I said that he was my superior in observation and deduction. If the art of the detective began and ended in reasoning from an arm-chair, my brother would be the greatest criminal agent that ever lived. But he has no ambition and no energy. He will not even go out of his way to verify his own solutions, and would rather be considered wrong than take the trouble to prove himself right. Again and again I have taken a problem to him, and have received an explanation which has afterwards proved to be the correct one. And yet he was absolutely incapable of working out the practical points which must be gone into before a case could be laid before a judge or jury."

Lots of talent, but "no ambition and no energy." We've all known people who have been blessed with certain gifts—a natural aptitude for music, great athletic skill—but chose not to develop those gifts. They ride along on pure talent, but talent only gets them so far. Holmes, while not as blessed as Mycroft, chose to exercise his mental muscles through rigorous and never-ending study, and as a result, he surpassed his older brother and became a living legend.

Based on a rigorous analysis of the habits of exceptional performers, the neurologist Daniel Levitin has estimated that it takes around ten thousand hours of practice over the course of a decade to develop into a truly world-class artist, musician, or athlete. Malcolm Gladwell refers to Levitin's research in his book *Outliers*, and goes on to point out that this ten-thousand-hour rule applies to everyone, even those we consider to be naturally gifted—the prodigies. The Beatles, chess player Bobby Fischer, Bill Gates—all of them devoted almost the same amount of time to their chosen profession before finally achieving mastery.

This is either exciting or depressing news, depending on your point of view. If you're just starting out in a particular field, it means you probably have a long, long way to go before you're truly considered to be the best at what you do. But at the same time, there's a silver lining, because the same rule appears to apply to everyone, regardless of whether you're born with a genetic advantage. Management guru Peter Drucker observed that at the end of the day, the measure of a person's effectiveness on the job has very little to do with their brainpower or imagination. He noted that highly intelligent men are usually "strikingly ineffectual" because they fail to harness and focus their talents.

Conan Doyle knew an awful lot about natural talent; after all, he came from a family of genuinely gifted artists, writers, and intellectuals. And yet somewhere along the way, he realized that talent wasn't enough. It's no surprise, then, that he created Sherlock Holmes, who embodies the best of both worlds—a natural genius who succeeds not solely because of his talent but because he combines his God-given gifts with hard work and a strong sense of purpose.

The choice is clear: You can become Mycroft or Sherlock. Everyone has a certain amount of natural talent in at least one area, regardless of whether it's baking, bicycling, or big business. The question is, what will you do with it?

Don't Take Yourself Too Seriously

> "Is there any point to which you would wish to draw my attention?"
>
> "To the curious incident of the dog in the night-time."
>
> "The dog did nothing in the night-time."
>
> "That was the curious incident," remarked Sherlock Holmes.
>
> —"SILVER BLAZE"

Conan Doyle spent a great deal of time and effort writing the Sherlock Holmes stories. The complex mysteries were woven together as intricately as tapestries and brought him a great deal of literary respect and critical acclaim.

However, he still maintained a healthy sense of humor about the whole enterprise. Despite the fact that he took his work seriously, he was able to laugh at himself and his wildly famous creation. Soon after Sherlock Holmes burst onto the literary scene, parodies and spoofs of the famous detective began to appear, usually lampooning Holmes's almost impossibly accurate detective skills and self-assuredness. One parody was even written by one of Conan Doyle's best friends,

J. M. Barrie, the author of *Peter Pan*! Conan Doyle liked it so much he reprinted it in a magazine article.

Rather than bristle at the potshots and take them as serious criticism, Conan Doyle went one step further and wrote two Sherlock Holmes parodies himself, one in 1896 and another in 1924. In both short stories he poked fun at the relationship between Holmes and Watson and even hinted that Watson was getting a little annoyed at his friend's constant displays of brilliance. And even though he had been careful to portray Watson as a strong and capable partner, he had no problem poking fun at the popular notion that the doctor was a somewhat befuddled guy. In "The Field Bazaar," his first parody, Holmes responds to one of Watson's questions this way:

[Holmes] smiled as he took his slipper from the mantelpiece and drew from it enough shag tobacco to fill the old clay pipe with which he invariably rounded off breakfast.

"A most characteristic question of yours, Watson," said he. "You will not, I am sure, be offended if I say that any reputation for sharpness which I may possess has been entirely gained by the admirable foil which you have made for me. Have I not heard of debutantes who have insisted on plainness in their chaperones? There is a certain analogy."

Later in the same parody, Holmes tells the doctor, "The fact is, my dear Watson, that you are an excellent subject. . . . You are never *blasé*. You respond instantly to any external stimulus. Your mental processes may be slow but they are never obscure, and I found during breakfast that you were easier reading than the [lead story] in the *Times* in front of me."

A healthy sense of humor can actually come in handy when you're faced with a problem or unexpected turn of events. Being able to see the humor in an otherwise tense situation helps you and everyone else around you remain loose and relaxed. As Henry Ward Beecher said, "A man without mirth is like a wagon without springs, in which one is caused disagreeably to jolt by every pebble over which it runs. A man with mirth is like a chariot with springs, in which one can ride over the roughest road, and scarcely feel anything but a pleasant rocking motion."

Maintaining your ability to see the funny side of life can also help keep you grounded after a big success when everyone is flattering you with compliments. Humble people are usually quick with a joke. Federal judge Harold R. Medina once quipped, "After all is said and done, we cannot deny the fact that a judge is almost of necessity surrounded by people who keep telling him what a wonderful fellow he is. And if he once begins to believe it, he is a lost soul."

In his later years, Conan Doyle often found himself in a similar situation, surrounded by admiring fans and Holmes devotees. By embracing the lighter side of his famous creation, and choosing to laugh along with the crowd rather than try in vain to defend Holmes from ridicule, he not only made his own life easier but improved his public image at the same time.

Develop Intense Concentration

Sherlock Holmes was transformed when he was hot upon such a scent as this.

—"THE BOSCOMBE VALLEY MYSTERY"

For some reason, many people believe that the ability to concentrate is a lot like good looks: You're either born with it or you're not. But in fact, concentration is a learned trait. With a little practice, anyone can hone their mind to a fixed point and block out the world around them.

If you want to succeed at any level, in any field—from sports to business to the arts—intense concentration is a must. Sherlock Holmes is a great role model in this respect, and Conan Doyle's description of the detective when he's hot on the trail of a criminal is a classic rendering of a motivated individual. Take this description from "The Boscombe Valley Mystery":

Sherlock Holmes was transformed when he was hot upon such a scent as this. Men who had only known the quiet thinker and logician of Baker Street would have failed to recognize him. His face flushed and darkened. His brows were drawn into two hard black lines, while his eyes shone out from beneath them with a steely glitter. His face was bent downward, his shoulders bowed, his lips compressed, and the veins stood out like whipcord in his long, sinewy neck. His nostrils seemed to dilate with a purely animal lust for the chase, and his mind was so absolutely concentrated upon the matter before him that a question or remark fell unheeded upon his ears, or, at the most, only provoked a quick, impatient snarl in reply.

As you can see, Sherlock Holmes was successful precisely because he could shut out everything else going on around him—the Scotland Yard detectives who secretly resented him and were constantly pressing him to solve their cases; the nervous victims; even Watson could get in the way at times. But Holmes persevered.

At the end of the day, we have a simple choice—but also an incredibly difficult one. Our conscious minds can dwell on only one thing at a time. Although we have two eyes, they work as a single unit—if one looks left, the other does, too. We were born with the innate ability to focus; in fact, it's im-

possible for us *not* to focus on something every waking minute. This can be a blessing or a curse. We can either train our
attention on what's important in our lives or what is extrane-
ous. The more you focus on your goals and passion, the easier
it is to keep that focus.

Admire Your Enemies

[Moriarty] is the Napoleon of crime, Watson. He is the organizer of half that is evil and of nearly all that is undetected in this great city. He is a genius, a philosopher, an abstract thinker. He has a brain of the first order.

—"THE FINAL PROBLEM"

Professor Moriarty, Sherlock Holmes's criminal nemesis, is almost as famous as the master detective, even though he appears only in a few of the later stories. What makes Moriarty such a great villain is that he is every bit the equal of Holmes and perhaps even surpasses him at times. Their rivalry is so compelling because the two are reverse-mirror images of the other, anticipating moves and countermoves like a pair of master chess players.

We face rivals at nearly every stage in our lives. In school, we compete against other athletes for a position on the basketball or football team or for the lead in the school play along with dozens of other hopefuls. Later on we compete against countless other teenagers across the country during the college admissions process. When we enter the business world, we find ourselves pitted against our official competitors at other companies. Sometimes our own coworkers can become enemies of a sort if there's a big promotion up for grabs. The same battle lines can be drawn in our personal lives, whether it's a PTA meeting or local neighborhood development organization.

Whatever the situation, rivals can stir up our emotions and cause us to act irrationally. If we find ourselves getting beaten badly in a competition or treated unfairly or cruelly, we can begin to feel sorry for ourselves or plot our revenge. Neither strategy is productive. Instead, we need to take a lesson from Holmes, even if it seems counterintuitive, and analyze our enemies objectively, even admiringly. It's the only way we'll eventually beat them.

Read the quote at the beginning of this chapter again. There is Holmes, actually gushing about the most evil villain he had ever faced. And yet his description is also 100 percent accurate and honest. Rather than try to find ways to denigrate Moriarty and boost his own ego, Holmes is clear-eyed about his opponent's talents; he doesn't try to make himself feel better by denigrating the other man's accomplishments. Why?

Because Holmes realizes that to win, he has to know his enemy inside and out. That means setting aside his own insecurities and admitting, yeah, the guy's good—*real* good. If Holmes is going to beat him, he'll have to step up his own game.

More than two thousand years ago, the Chinese master strategist Sun Tzu wrote in the now-classic *The Art of War*, "If you know the enemy and know yourself, you need not fear the result of a hundred battles. If you know yourself but not the enemy, for every victory gained you will also suffer a defeat. If you know neither the enemy nor yourself, you will succumb in every battle."

It's fun to slag on our enemies and make jokes about them, but it doesn't get us any closer to conquering them. If you're facing a formidable challenger, don't focus on their grating voice or that self-satisfied smirk that drives you up the wall. Analyze their actual skills and talents. What makes them so dangerous, so hard to beat? What are their greatest talents, their specialties? If you were their friend, how would you describe them to someone else? Make a list. You may find that they're not as powerful as you thought they were. On the other hand, conducting an assessment like this may make you realize they're even *more* powerful than you first suspected. Either way, the outcome is positive—if someone invited you to participate in a boxing match, wouldn't you want to know the nature of your opponent before you accepted? Focusing on your enemy in a clear, rational way gives you knowledge you didn't have before—and that's the first step in developing a successful strategy to engage him or her on the battlefield.

Be Your Own Librarian

[Holmes] had a horror of destroying documents, especially
those which were connected with his past cases, and yet it was
only once in every year or two that he would muster energy to
docket and arrange them.

—"THE MUSGRAVE RITUAL"

Everyone knows that we're supposed to look forward to the
future, not get stuck in the past. But in reality, the ways in
which we choose to remember our prior actions can have a
huge influence on our lives.

Holmes was a pack rat, but not an indiscriminate one; he
held on to only the things he thought were truly valuable. In
"The Musgrave Ritual," Watson describes Holmes's office:

Thus month after month his papers accumulated, until
every corner of the room was stacked with bundles of man-
uscript which were on no account to be burned, and which
could not be put away save by their owner. One winter's

night, as we sat together by the fire, I ventured to suggest
to him that, as he had finished pasting extracts into his
common-place book, he might employ the next two hours
in making our room a little more habitable. He could not
deny the justice of my request, so with a rather rueful face
he went off to his bedroom, from which he returned pres-
ently pulling a large tin box behind him. This he placed in
the middle of the floor and, squatting down upon a stool
in front of it, he threw back the lid. I could see that it was
already a third full of bundles of paper tied up with red
tape into separate packages.

His habit of keeping every scrap of paper associated with
his old cases is a telling detail. For one thing, maintaining
accurate records is simply good business practice, especially
for an entrepreneur like Holmes. But his treasure trove of
papers also served as proof of his success—a kind of psychological reinforcement, similar to the way executives and doctors hang their diplomas and credentials on their office walls.
His tin box filled with old case files reminded him of how far
he had come, and they also served as valuable research material that could assist him in new cases.

Like Holmes, we should be *selective* pack rats when it comes
to our past. Performance psychologists have found that high
achievers—athletes, businessmen, movie stars—have a short-

term memory when it comes to failures, but a long-term memory for their successes. Star basketball players don't dwell on bad games or spend hours replaying every missed shot or double dribble. However, they consciously choose to remember their past glories—the great three-point jumper from half-court, the MVP trophy at the end of the season—and oftentimes replay them in their heads during training, like a highlight reel on an endless loop.

This is not to say that we should block out all negative memories. We need to think hard about the serious mistakes we make so we can avoid them in the future. Holmes confided to Watson that not all of his records were of successful cases. No doubt he had a few real stinkers in that tin box as well, but he used them in the right way: as a healthy reminder not to make certain errors in the future.

What's in your tin box? Is it filled with regrets and catalogs of past mistakes, or are you being careful to fill it up with memories that will motivate you and help you achieve your goals?

Master Your Allusions

**You remind me of Edgar Allan Poe's Dupin. I had no idea that
such individuals did exist out of stories.**

—WATSON, IN *A STUDY IN SCARLET*

Part of the fun of reading the Sherlock Holmes tales is ferret-
ing out the tiny details Conan Doyle was fond of inserting
into the adventures. He was widely read, so he constantly
threw in quotations from and allusions to great works of literature and philosophy, from quoting Goethe in the original
German in *The Sign of Four* (translated as "Nature alas, made
only one being of you although there was material for a good
man and a rogue") to Shakespeare ("The game is afoot!" from
Henry V) in "The Adventure of the Abbey Grange," and

making references to a plethora of other writers, from Thoreau and Darwin to Horace and Dickens. Almost all of the quotes are uttered by Holmes, which was no accident; to flesh out the character, Conan Doyle made sure that when his brilliant sleuth alluded to a statement from someone else, it was equally brilliant.

The same principle works in real life. Our allusions—the words and phrases that spring to mind in certain situations—say more about us than we realize. What would you think if your boss went around all day quoting lines from old episodes of *The Flintstones*, for instance? Or what if, every time you asked a question, he responded with a catchphrase from an old fast-food commercial? Likewise, what if Holmes had walked around London quoting cartoons from the newspaper or crude jokes from the latest bawdy stage show? It would have had a profound effect on how we, the readers, viewed him (not to mention his clients!).

Holmes's allusions always reflected his rigorous self-education and rarified position as a genius of criminal detection. Quoting Shakespeare, for instance, was congruent with his public image, the "brand" he used to attract clients and build his business. Our attitude, choice of conversation topics, and, yes, our allusions—literary or otherwise—all send out subtle signals about our professional competence and our ability to work with others. This is good news, because it gives us a great deal of say in how we will be perceived.

Several years ago, I heard a famous author give a speech about a rather strange subject—extraterrestrials. He was well-spoken, well-educated, and fervently believed that aliens were real. One of the highlights of his talk was the recounting of an alleged alien abduction in South America. He told the story with such passion and mastery of the details that when he was finished, I found myself almost completely convinced that . . . well . . . *something* had happened.

A few weeks later I was sitting in a barbershop waiting to get a haircut. Bored, I picked up a months-old copy of a tabloid newspaper from the seat next to me and began flipping through it. Lo and behold, on page twenty-three, I found an article about the very same alleged alien abduction. As I read it, I recognized nearly every detail the speaker had used during his presentation. He had used a tabloid as his primary source of information.

Now, what do you think happened to my impression of the author? It tanked, of course! I couldn't believe he had chosen to build an entire argument based on a questionable story in a newspaper that frequently ran claims about Bigfoot secretly controlling the outcome of *American Idol*. His choice of subject matter—and that allusion to the tabloid story—had destroyed his credibility.

We shouldn't pretend to be someone we're not in order to to get ahead. At the same time, there's nothing wrong with thinking carefully about what we say and how we say it in certain situations. Our words can make or break our reputation. Just ask Sherlock Holmes.

Never Stop Encouraging

"And that recommendation," [Holmes recalled to Watson . . .]
"was, if you will believe me, Watson, the very first thing which
ever made me feel that a profession might be made out of what
had up to that time been the merest hobby."
—"THE ADVENTURE OF THE 'GLORIA SCOTT'"

Have you ever wondered how Sherlock Holmes got his start as
a detective? Conan Doyle purposely revealed very little about
Holmes's early life, but in one story, "The Adventure of the
'Gloria Scott,'" we get a rare and insightful glimpse into his
beginnings.

The story begins with Holmes recalling his time in college (he stayed only two years before dropping out). His only
friend was a man named Victor Trevor. Once, when Holmes
was around twenty, Victor invited him to his father's estate
for a monthlong vacation.

At that time, Holmes said he was "rather fond of moping
in my rooms and working out my own little methods of

thought," but he decided to go anyway. "One evening, shortly after my arrival," Holmes recalled, "we were sitting over a glass of port after dinner, when young Trevor began to talk about those habits of observation and inference which I had already formed into a system, although I had not yet appreciated the part which they were to play in my life. The old man evidently thought that his son was exaggerating in his description of one or two trivial feats which I had performed."

Holmes couldn't resist the challenge. He trained his powers of deduction on Victor's father and accurately described the provenance of his walking stick, revealed that the man was once a boxer and had traveled to both New Zealand and Japan—all without leaving the table. The old man was so astonished that he fainted dead away. When he came round, he said something that would forever change the life of the young Holmes: "I don't know how you manage this, Mr. Holmes, but it seems to me that all the detectives of fact and of fancy would be children in your hands. That's your line of life, sir, and you may take the word of a man who has seen something of the world."

"And that recommendation," Holmes recalled to Watson, "with the exaggerated estimate of my ability with which he prefaced it, was, if you will believe me, Watson, the very first thing which ever made me feel that a profession might be made out of what had up to that time been the merest hobby."

In other words, it was the errant comment of a stranger that convinced Holmes he might be able to make a living out of his greatest passion. Until that point, he had never even considered that such a thing was possible. In a way, Trevor's father could claim a share of the credit for everything Holmes accomplished after that point.

Encouragement can come from anywhere at any time. A few words spoken at the right time can alter a person's career trajectory and open up a new world of possibilities. Holmes learned this lesson too—he constantly encouraged Watson to learn his methods of detection and apply them to the case at hand.

Words have power, regardless of their source. Choose yours carefully, and the next time you notice someone's talent, tell him. Who knows? It might be the first time someone has pointed out his own genius to him.

The Sherlock Holmes Success Lexicon

Arthur Conan Doyle wasn't just a legendary mystery writer—he also had an ingenious knack for creating pithy, memorable quotes for his greatest literary creation, Sherlock Holmes. Indeed, many Holmes quotations are still a part of the pop-culture lexicon more than a century after they were first written.

There are many collections of Sherlock Holmes's greatest hits floating around the Internet, but the majority of them recycle the same handful of quotes over and over—usually mixed together with a few not-so-great quotes—and in no particular order. Worse yet, often they don't tell you from which particular story each quote was taken.

The collection that follows is very different. I've compiled a number of Sherlock Holmes quotations, only some of which are found elsewhere in this book, to illustrate and amplify the subjects discussed in earlier chapters. The quotes are arranged by topic, so you can quickly find the ones that best fit your needs. Write them out on index cards and tape them to your cubicle wall or refrigerator door; pin them to the bulletin board that hangs over your computer. Use them as constant reminders that you too can emulate the greatest detective that never lived!

Focus and Single-Mindedness

A man should keep his little brain attic stocked with all the furniture that he is likely to use, and the rest he can put away in the lumber-room of his library, where he can get it if he wants it.

—"The Five Orange Pips"

"You see," [Holmes] explained. "I consider that a man's brain originally is like a little empty attic, and you have to stock it with such furniture as you choose. A fool takes in all the lumber of every sort that he comes across, so that the knowledge which might be useful to him gets crowded out, or at best is jumbled up with a lot of other things, so that he has a difficulty in laying his hands upon it. Now the skillful workman is very careful indeed as to what he takes into his brain-attic. He will have nothing but the tools which may help him in doing his work, but of these he has a large assortment, and all in the most perfect order. It is a mistake to think that little room has elastic walls and can distend to any extent. Depend upon it there comes a time when for every addition of knowledge you forget something that you knew before. It is of the highest importance, therefore, not to have useless facts elbowing out the useful ones."

—*A Study in Scarlet*

[Holmes] said that he would acquire no knowledge which did not bear upon his object.

—*A Study in Scarlet*

It is not so impossible, however, that a man should possess all knowledge which is likely to be useful to him in his work, and this, I have endeavored in my case to do.

—"The Five Orange Pips"

My name is Sherlock Holmes. It is my business to know what other people don't know.

—"The Adventure of the Blue Carbuncle"

To let the brain work without sufficient material is like racing an engine. It racks itself to pieces.

—"The Adventure of the Devil's Foot"

Motivation

I cannot live without brain-work. What else is there to live for?

—*The Sign of Four*

There is nothing more stimulating than a case where everything goes against you.

—*The Hound of the Baskervilles*

"My mind," he said, "rebels at stagnation. Give me problems, give me work, give me the most abstruse cryptogram, or the most intricate analysis, and I am in my own proper atmosphere. . . . But I abhor the dull routine of existence. I crave for mental exaltation. That is why I have chosen my own particular profession, or rather created it, for I am the only one in the world."

—*The Sign of Four*

My dear Watson, you know how bored I have been since we locked up Colonel Carruthers. My mind is like a racing engine, tearing itself to pieces because it is not connected up with the work for which it was built. Life is commonplace; the papers are sterile; audacity and romance seem to have passed forever from the criminal world. Can you ask me, then, whether I am ready to look into any new problem, however trivial it may prove?

—"The Adventure of Wisteria Lodge"

I am the last and highest court of appeal in detection. When Gregson, or Lestrade, or Athelney Jones are out of their depths—which, by the way, is their normal state—the matter is laid before me. I examine the data, as an expert, and pronounce a specialist's opinion. I claim no credit in such cases. My name figures in no newspaper. The work itself, the pleasure of finding a field for my peculiar powers, is my highest reward.

—*The Sign of Four*

Chance has put in our way a most singular and whimsical problem, and its solution is its own reward.

—"The Adventure of the Blue Carbuncle"

Holmes, however, like all great artists, lived for his art's sake. . . . He frequently refused his help to the powerful and wealthy where the problem made no appeal to his sympathies, while he would devote weeks of most intense application to the affairs of some humble client whose case presented those strange and dramatic qualities which appealed to his imagination and challenged his ingenuity.

—"The Adventure of Black Peter"

On glancing over my notes of the seventy odd cases in which I have during the last eight years studied the methods of my friend Sherlock Holmes, I find many tragic, some comic, a large number merely strange, but none commonplace; for, working as he did rather for the love of his art than for the acquirement of wealth, he refused to associate himself with any investigation which did not tend towards the unusual, and even the fantastic.

—"The Adventure of the Speckled Band"

Sherlock Holmes was transformed when he was hot upon such a scent as this. Men who had only known the quiet thinker and logician of Baker Street would have failed to recognize him. His face flushed and darkened. His brows were drawn into two hard black lines, while his eyes shone out from beneath them with a steely glitter. His face was bent downward, his shoulders bowed, his lips compressed, and the veins stood out like whipcord in his long, sinewy neck. His nostrils seemed to dilate with a purely animal lust for the chase, and his mind was so absolutely concentrated upon the matter before him that a question or remark fell unheeded upon his ears, or, at the most, only provoked a quick, impatient snarl in reply.

—"The Boscombe Valley Mystery"

"Tut! tut!" cried Sherlock Holmes. "You must act, man, or you are lost. Nothing but energy can save you. This is no time for despair."

—"The Five Orange Pips"

Figuring Out Tough Problems

Let us take it link by link.

—"The Adventure of Wisteria Lodge"

In solving a problem of this sort, the grand thing is to be able to reason backward. That is a very useful accomplishment, and a very easy one, but people do not practice it much. In the everyday affairs of life it is more useful to reason forward, and so the other comes to be neglected. There are fifty who can reason synthetically for one who can reason analytically.

—*A Study in Scarlet*

The more outré and grotesque an incident is the more carefully it deserves to be examined, and the very point which appears to complicate a case is, when duly considered and scientifically handled, the one which is most likely to elucidate it.

—*The Hound of the Baskervilles*

My whole examination served to turn my conjecture into a certainty.

—"The Adventure of the Noble Bachelor"

"The case has been an interesting one," remarked Holmes when our visitors had left us, "because it serves to show very clearly how simple the explanation may be of an affair which at first sight seems to be almost inexplicable. Nothing could be more natural than the sequence of events as narrated by this lady, and nothing stranger than the result when viewed, for instance, by Mr. Lestrade, of Scotland Yard."

—"The Adventure of the Noble Bachelor"

"I will not bias your mind by suggesting theories or suspicions, Watson," said he; "I wish you simply to report facts in the fullest possible manner to me, and you can leave me to do the theorizing."

—*The Hound of the Baskervilles*

From a drop of water . . . a logician could infer the possibility of an Atlantic or a Niagara without having seen or heard of one or the other. So all life is a great chain, the nature of which is known whenever we are shown a single link of it. Like all other arts, the Science of Deduction and Analysis is one which can only be acquired by long and patient study, nor is life long enough to allow any mortal to attain the highest possible perfection in it. Before turning to those moral and mental aspects of the matter which present the greatest difficulties, let the enquirer begin by mastering more elementary problems. Let him, on meeting a fellow-mortal, learn at a glance to distinguish the history of the man, and the trade or profession to which he belongs. Puerile as such an exercise may seem, it sharpens the faculties of observation, and teaches one where to look and what to look for. By a man's finger nails, by his coat-sleeve, by his boot, by his trouser knees, by the callosities of his forefinger and thumb, by his expression, by his shirt cuffs—

by each of these things a man's calling is plainly revealed. That all united should fail to enlighten the competent enquirer in any case is almost inconceivable.

—A Study in Scarlet

How often have I said to you that when you have eliminated the impossible, whatever remains, however improbable, must be the truth?

—The Sign of Four

"Ah, that is good luck. I could only say what was the balance of probability. I did not at all expect to be so accurate."

"But it was not mere guesswork?"

"No, no: I never guess. It is a shocking habit—destructive to the logical faculty. What seems strange to you is only so because you do not follow my train of thought or observe the small facts upon which large inferences may depend."

—The Sign of Four

"It is of the first importance," he cried, "not to allow your judgment to be biased by personal qualities. A client is to me a mere unit, a factor in a problem. The emotional qualities are antagonistic to clear reasoning. I assure you that the most winning woman I ever knew was hanged for poisoning three little children for their insurance-money, and the most repellent man of my acquaintance is a philanthropist who has spent nearly a quarter of a million upon the London poor."

—*The Sign of Four*

As Cuvier could correctly describe a whole animal by the contemplation of a single bone, so the observer who has thoroughly understood one link in a series of incidents should be able to accurately state all the other ones, both before and after.

—"The Five Orange Pips"

At least I have got a grip of the essential facts of the case. I shall enumerate them to you, for nothing clears up a case so much as stating it to another person, and I can hardly expect your cooperation if I do not show you the position from which we start.

—"Silver Blaze"

Any truth is better than indefinite doubt.

—"The Yellow Face"

Perhaps, when a man has special knowledge and special powers like my own, it rather encourages him to seek a complex explanation when a simpler one is at hand.

—"The Adventure of the Abbey Grange"

I have devised seven separate explanations, each of which would cover the facts as far as we know them. But which of these is correct can only be determined by the fresh information which we shall no doubt find waiting for us.

—"The Adventure of the Copper Beeches"

"We are coming now rather into the region of guesswork," said Dr. Mortimer.

"Say, rather, into the region where we balance probabilities and choose the most likely. It is the scientific use of the imagination, but we have always some material basis on which to start our speculation."

—*The Hound of the Baskervilles*

Attention to Detail

You see, but you do not observe. The distinction is clear.

—"A Scandal in Bohemia"

It has long been an axiom of mine that the little things are infinitely the most important.

—"A Case of Identity"

You know my method. It is founded upon the observation of trifles.

—"The Boscombe Valley Mystery"

On the contrary, Watson, you can see everything. You fail, however, to reason from what you see. You are too timid in drawing your inferences.

—"The Adventure of the Blue Carbuncle"

It is, of course, a trifle, but there is nothing so important as trifles.

—"The Man with the Twisted Lip"

"I am glad of all details," remarked my friend, "whether they seem to you to be relevant or not."

—"The Adventure of the Copper Beeches"

"You have an extraordinary genius for minutiae," I remarked.

—*The Sign of Four*

Never trust to general impressions, my boy, but concentrate yourself upon details.

—"A Case of Identity"

The world is full of obvious things which nobody by any chance ever observes.

—*The Hound of the Baskervilles*

"If I take it up I must understand every detail," said [Holmes]. "Take time to consider. The smallest point may be the most essential."

—"The Adventure of the Red Circle"

"By George!" cried the inspector. "How ever did you see that?"

"Because I looked for it," [Holmes said].

—"The Adventure of the Dancing Men"

Qualities of a Genius

"They say that genius is an infinite capacity for taking pains," he remarked with a smile. "It's a very bad definition, but it does apply to detective work."

—*A Study in Scarlet*

Appendix

[Holmes] is a little queer in his ideas—an enthusiast in some branches of science.

—A Study in Scarlet

One of Sherlock Holmes's defects—if, indeed, one may call it a defect—was that he was exceedingly loath to communicate his full plans to any other person until the instant of their fulfillment. Partly it came no doubt from his own masterful nature, which loved to dominate and surprise those who were around him. Partly also from his professional caution, which urged him never to take any chances. The result, however, was very trying for those who were acting as his agents and assistants.

—The Hound of the Baskervilles

[Holmes's] studies are very desultory and eccentric, but he has amassed a lot of out-of-the-way knowledge which would astonish his professors.

—A Study in Scarlet

[Holmes] appears to have a passion for definite and exact knowledge.

—A Study in Scarlet

Sherlock Holmes's smallest actions were all directed towards some definite and practical end.

—A Study in Scarlet

"Never mind," said Holmes, laughing; "it is my business to know things. Perhaps I have trained myself to see what others overlook. If not, why should you come to consult me?"

—"A Case of Identity"

Making Good Decisions

It is a capital mistake to theorize before you have all the evidence. It biases the judgment.

—*A Study in Scarlet*

When a fact appears to be opposed to a long train of deductions, it invariably proves to be capable of bearing some other interpretation.

—*A Study in Scarlet*

It is a capital mistake to theorize before one has data. Insensibly one begins to twist facts to suit theories, instead of theories to suit facts.

—"A Scandal in Bohemia"

"Circumstantial evidence is a very tricky thing," answered Holmes thoughtfully. "It may seem to point very straight to one thing, but if you shift your own point of view a little, you may find it pointing in an equally uncompromising manner to something entirely different."

—"The Boscombe Valley Mystery"

Singularity is almost invariably a clue. The more feature-less and commonplace a crime is, the more difficult it is to bring it home.

—"The Boscombe Valley Mystery"

There is nothing more deceptive than an obvious fact.

—"The Boscombe Valley Mystery"

It is an old maxim of mine that when you have excluded the impossible, whatever remains, however improbable, must be the truth.

—"The Adventure of the Beryl Coronet"

"Data! data! data!" he cried impatiently. "I can't make bricks without clay."

—"The Adventure of the Copper Beeches"

"I had," said [Holmes], "come to an entirely erroneous conclusion which shows, my dear Watson, how dangerous it always is to reason from insufficient data."

—"The Adventure of the Speckled Band"

It is of the highest importance in the art of detection to be able to recognize, out of a number of facts, which are incidental and which vital. Otherwise your energy and attention must be dissipated instead of being concentrated.

—"The Reigate Puzzle"

You did not know where to look, and so you missed all that was important.

—"A Case of Identity"

Giving Your Mind a Rest

It is quite a three pipe problem, and I beg that you won't speak to me for fifty minutes.

—"The Red-Headed League"

I knew that seclusion and solitude were very necessary for my friend in those hours of intense mental concentration during which he weighed every particle of evidence, constructed alternative theories, balanced one against the other, and made up his mind as to which points were essential and which immaterial.

—*The Hound of the Baskervilles*

Well, I gave my mind a thorough rest by plunging into a chemical analysis. One of our greatest statesmen has said that a change of work is the best rest. So it is.

—The Sign of Four

One of the most remarkable characteristics of Sherlock Holmes was his power of throwing his brain out of action and switching all his thoughts on to lighter things whenever he had convinced himself that he could no longer work to advantage.

—"The Adventure of the Bruce-Partington Plans"

Sherlock Holmes had, in a very remarkable degree, the power of detaching his mind at will. For two hours the strange business in which we had been involved appeared to be forgotten.

—The Hound of the Baskervilles

References

SECRET 1: "A PASSION FOR DEFINITE AND EXACT KNOWLEDGE"

Robert Christison, *The Life of Sir Robert Christison, Bart.* (Edinburgh and London: William Blackwood and Sons, 1886), 115–116.

SECRET 3: "AN EXTRAORDINARY GENIUS FOR MINUTIAE"

Raymond Blathwayt, "A Talk with Dr. Conan Doyle," *Bookman*, May 1892.

Thomas Wright, *Hind Head: Or the English Switzerland and Its Literary and Historical Associations* (London: Simpkin, Marshall, Hamilton, Kent & Company Ltd., 1898), 12.

SECRET 4: "A CAPITAL MISTAKE"

"Recreations of a Philosopher," *Harper's New Monthly Magazine*, December 1864, 37.

SECRET 5: FEED YOUR PASSION

Robin Miller, "Ray Bradbury: Following His Passion to Mars," *Town Talk*, February 2000, www.raybradbury.com/articles_town_talk .html.

SECRET 6: "A LITTLE EMPTY ATTIC"

Henry Foster Adams, "Psychology Goldbricks," *Scribner's Magazine*, June 1921, 658.
Frank Crane, *Four Minute Essays*, vol. 8 (New York/Chicago: William H. Wise & Company, 1919), 147.

SECRET 8: "LET US CALMLY DEFINE OUR POSITION"

Sir Arthur Conan Doyle, *Sir Arthur Conan Doyle: Adventures and Memories* (London: Wordsworth Editions, 2007), 33.

SECRET 9: THE ONLY RULE IS THAT THERE ARE NO RULES

Harry How, "A Day with Dr. Conan Doyle," *Strand Magazine*, vol. IV, July to December 1892 (London: George Newnes Ltd., 1892), 183.

SECRET 12: APPROACH PROBLEMS WITH A BLANK MIND

William Rivers Taylor, *The Spiritual Life of the Business Man* (Rochester: Ernest Hart, 1908), 32.

SECRET 15: EVERYTHING IS USEFUL

Sidney Colvin, ed., *The Letters of Robert Louis Stevenson*, vol. 2 (New York: Scribners, 1899), 341.

Sir Arthur Conan Doyle, *Through the Magic Door* (London: Smith, Elder & Company, 1907), 255.

SECRET 16: FIND THE RIGHT WATSON

Ben Macintyre, "Can I Be Complimentary, My Dear Watson?" *London Times*, Dec. 17, 2009, www.timesonline.co.uk/tol/comment/colum nists/ben_macintyre/article6959515.ece.

"Jeremy Brett: Interview," *Fifty-Four*, http://gunner54.wordpress.com/ jeremy-brett-interview/.

References

SECRET 21: HONOR YOUR TEACHERS

Marcus Aurelius, *The Thoughts of the Emperor Marcus Aurelius Antoninus*, trans. George Long (Boston: Little, Brown and Company, 1892), 81–82.

SECRET 22: MIMIC THE METHOD

E. A. Greening Lamborn, "The Methods of Sherlock Holmes in Nature-Study," *Nature-Study Review*, May 1905, 124–125.
"The Method of Sherlock Holmes in Medicine," *The Medical Bulletin*, vol. 22 (Philadelphia: F. A. Davis Company, 1900), 70.

SECRET 23: PICTURE YOUR DREAMS AS REALITY

Sir Arthur Conan Doyle, *The Complete Sherlock Holmes*, vol. II (New York: Barnes & Noble Classics, 2003), 692.

SECRET 24: REBEL AT STAGNATION

Harry How, "A Day with Dr. Conan Doyle," *Strand Magazine*, vol. IV, July to December 1892 (London: George Newnes Ltd., 1892), 185, 187.

SECRET 26: TALENT ISN'T ENOUGH

Peter Drucker, *The Essential Drucker* (Oxford: Elsevier Ltd., 2007), 145.

SECRET 27: DON'T TAKE YOURSELF TOO SERIOUSLY

Henry Ward Beecher, *Royal Truths* (Edinburgh: Alexander Strahan & Company, 1862), 241–242.

Edward Devitt, "Ten Commandments for the New Judge," *ABA Journal*, December 1961, 1175.

Index

Index

Index

Index

About the Author

David Acord is the author of *What Would Lincoln Do? Lincoln's Most Inspired Solutions to Challenging Problems and Difficult Situations.* He lives and works in Arlington, Virginia.